Jane Eyre

THE GRAPHIC NOVEL
Charlotte Brontë

ORIGINAL TEXT VERSION

Script Adaptation: Amy Corzine
Artwork: John M. Burns
Lettering: Terry Wiley
Design & Layout: Jo Wheeler & Carl Andrews
Publishing Assistant: Joanna Watts
Additional Information: Karen Wenborn

Editor in Chief: Clive Bryant

Jane Eyre: The Graphic Novel
Original Text Version

Charlotte Brontë

First UK Edition

Published by: Classical Comics Ltd
Copyright ©2008 Classical Comics Ltd.

Acknowledgments: Every effort has been made to trace copyright holders of
material reproduced in this book. Any rights not acknowledged here will be
acknowledged in subsequent editions if notice is given to Classical Comics Ltd.

All enquiries should be addressed to:
Classical Comics Ltd.
PO Box 7280
Litchborough
Towcester
NN12 9AR
United Kingdom
Tel: 0845 812 3000

info@classicalcomics.com
www.classicalcomics.com

ISBN: 978-1-906332-06-8

Printed in the UK

This book is printed by Hampton Printing (Bristol) Ltd using biodegradable vegetable inks, on
environmentally friendly paper which is FSC (Forest Stewardship Council) certified (TT-COC-002370) and
manufactured to the accredited Environmental Management Standard ISO 14001. This material can be
disposed of by recycling, incineration for energy recovery, composting and biodegradation.

Mixed Sources
Product group from well-managed
forests and other controlled sources
www.fsc.org Cert no. TT-COC-002370
FSC © 1996 Forest Stewardship Council

The publishers would like to acknowledge the
design assistance of Greg Powell in the completion of this book.

Contents

Dramatis Personae

Jane Eyre

Mr. Edward Fairfax Rochester
Owner of Thornfield Hall

Young Jane Eyre

Mr. Reed
Jane's uncle

Mrs. Sarah Reed
Jane's aunt

John Reed
Jane's cousin

Eliza Reed
Jane's cousin

Georgiana Reed
Jane's cousin

Miss Bessie Lee
Maid at Gateshead Hall

Miss Abbott
Maid at Gateshead Hall

Mr. Lloyd
Apothecary

Mr. Brocklehurst
Manager of Lowood School

Miss Maria Temple
*Superintendent at
Lowood School*

Helen Burns
*Jane's friend at
Lowood School*

Miss Alice Fairfax
*Housekeeper at
Thornfield Hall*

Adèle Varens
Jane's pupil

Céline Varens
Adele's mother

Grace Poole
Maid at Gateshead Hall

Lord Ingram

Lady Ingram

Miss Blanche Ingram
*Daughter of Lord and
Lady Ingram*

Miss Mary Ingram
*Daughter of Lord and
Lady Ingram*

**Bertha Mason
Rochester**

Richard Mason
Bertha's brother

Mr. Briggs
A solicitor from London

Pilot
Mr. Rochester's dog

St. John Rivers

Mary Rivers
Sister to St. John

Diana Rivers
Sister to St. John

Rosamond Oliver
Friend of St. John Rivers

The Birth of Jane Eyre

Charlotte Brontë's *Jane Eyre* was a huge success when it first appeared in 1847. It was a year of great achievement for the Brontë sisters of Haworth: the publication of Anne Brontë's *Agnes Grey*, and Emily Brontë's *Wuthering Heights* also taking place that same year.

That success, however, was set against a family history full of loss and sadness.

Despite the many advances made in medical science during the nineteenth century, potentially fatal diseases were still extremely common. Charlotte had to cope with her mother's death when she was only five years old; and then, four years later, two of her sisters were lost to tuberculosis.

Young Charlotte was fortunate enough to have a caring father and aunt to look after her – but what about an infant who had lost both parents?

It was usual for orphaned children to be looked after by relatives; and while the kindness of that act cannot be denied, the emotional impact of the loss of parents on the child, coupled with the stresses felt by the family looking after an extra person in the household, could provide the background to an unhappy childhood – especially for a poor, plain little girl, thrust into the home of her spiteful cousins and an uncaring aunt.

Jane Eyre

~ PROLOGUE ~

NORTHERN ENGLAND IN THE EARLY NINETEENTH CENTURY

NOW THAT *TYPHUS* HAS FELLED BOTH MY *SISTER* AND HER *HUSBAND*, WE MUST LOOK AFTER THEIR *CHILD.*

REVEREND EYRE

WIFE TO REVEREND EYRE

GATESHEAD HALL

ONE YEAR LATER...

PROMISE ME, MRS. REED, TO REAR AND MAINTAIN LITTLE *JANE EYRE* AS ONE OF OUR *OWN* CHILDREN.

I *WILL,* HUSBAND.

CHAPTER I

NINE YEARS LATER...

NO LONG **WALK** TODAY, SO NO **NIPPED** FINGERS AND TOES.

I REGRET TO KEEP YOU AT A **DISTANCE**, JANE,

BUT UNTIL I HAVE HEARD FROM THE **NURSEMAID**, BESSIE --

I **LIKE** IT WHEN **BESSIE** TELLS ME **STORIES**

-- THAT YOU ARE **ENDEAVOURING** IN **GOOD EARNEST** TO ACQUIRE A MORE **SOCIABLE** AND **CHILDLIKE DISPOSITION** --

-- A MORE **ATTRACTIVE** AND **SPRIGHTLY** MANNER

- SOMETHING **LIGHTER, FRANKER,** MORE **NATURAL** -

I REALLY **MUST** EXCLUDE YOU FROM **PRIVILEGES** INTENDED ONLY FOR **CONTENTED, HAPPY** LITTLE CHILDREN.

WHAT DOES **BESSIE** SAY I HAVE **DONE**?

JANE, I DON'T LIKE **CAVILLERS** OR **QUESTIONERS**; BESIDES, THERE IS SOMETHING TRULY **FORBIDDING** IN A **CHILD** TAKING UP HER **ELDERS** IN THAT MANNER.

BE SEATED SOMEWHERE; AND UNTIL YOU CAN SPEAK **PLEASANTLY,**

REMAIN **SILENT.**

9

BOH! MADAM MOPE!...

WHERE THE DICKENS IS SHE?

IT IS WELL I DREW THE CURTAIN

LIZZY! GEORGY!

JOAN* IS NOT HERE:

TELL MAMA SHE IS RUN OUT INTO THE RAIN --

-- BAD ANIMAL!

SHE IS IN THE WINDOW-SEAT, TO BE SURE, JACK.

WHAT DO YOU WANT?

SAY: "WHAT DO YOU WANT, MASTER REED?"

THAT WAS THE ANSWER!

I WANT YOU TO COME HERE --

-- THAT IS FOR YOUR IMPUDENCE IN ANSWERING MAMA A WHILE BACK --

SMACK

-- AND FOR YOUR SNEAKING WAY OF GETTING BEHIND CURTAINS, AND FOR THE LOOK YOU HAD IN YOUR EYES TWO MINUTES SINCE, YOU RAT!

WHAT WERE YOU DOING BEHIND THE CURTAIN?

I WAS READING.

10

*Master Reed would often call her Joan.

SHOW THE BOOK. --

YOU ARE A **DEPENDENT,** MAMA SAYS; YOU HAVE NO **MONEY.** YOU OUGHT TO **BEG,** NOT LIVE WITH **GENTLEMAN'S CHILDREN** LIKE **US,** AND EAT THE SAME **MEALS** WE DO, AND WEAR **CLOTHES** AT OUR **MAMMA'S EXPENSE** --

-- YOU HAVE NO **BUSINESS** TO TAKE OUR **BOOKS;**

-- **NOW** I'LL TEACH YOU TO RUMMAGE MY **BOOKSHELVES,** FOR THEY ARE **MINE.** ALL THE HOUSE BELONGS TO ME, OR **WILL** DO.

GO AND STAND BY THE **DOOR,** OUT OF THE WAY OF THE **MIRROR** AND THE **WINDOWS.**

AAH!

THUMP!

WICKED AND **CRUEL** BOY!

YOU ARE LIKE A **MURDERER,** A **SLAVE-DRIVER** --

-- YOU ARE LIKE THE **ROMAN EMPERORS!**

WHAT! WHAT! DID YOU **HEAR** HER, **ELIZA** AND **GEORGIANA?**

WON'T I TELL **MAMA!** BUT **FIRST** --

RAT!

RAT!

MAMA!

MAMA!

DEAR, DEAR! WHAT A *FURY* TO FLY AT *MASTER JOHN!*

DID ANYBODY SEE SUCH A *PICTURE* OF *PASSION?*

TAKE HER AWAY TO THE *RED-ROOM* AND *LOCK HER* IN THERE.

~ CHAPTER II ~

FOR *SHAME*, FOR *SHAME!*

WHAT *SHOCKING CONDUCT*, MISS EYRE, TO *STRIKE* YOUR YOUNG *MASTER!*

MASTER! HOW IS HE MY *MASTER?* AM I A *SERVANT?*

NO, YOU ARE *LESS* THAN A SERVANT, FOR YOU DO *NOTHING* FOR YOUR *KEEP.*

12

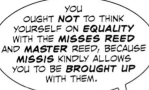

YOU OUGHT **NOT** TO THINK YOURSELF ON **EQUALITY** WITH THE **MISSES REED** AND **MASTER** REED, BECAUSE **MISSIS** KINDLY ALLOWS YOU TO BE **BROUGHT UP** WITH THEM.

THEY WILL HAVE A **GREAT DEAL** OF **MONEY** AND YOU WILL HAVE **NONE.** IT IS YOUR **PLACE** TO MAKE YOURSELF **AGREEABLE** TO THEM.

WHAT WE TELL YOU IS FOR YOUR **OWN GOOD.**

IF **MRS. REED** WERE TO **TURN YOU OUT,** YOU WOULD HAVE TO GO TO THE **POORHOUSE.**

COME BESSIE, WE WILL **LEAVE** HER --

-- I WOULDN'T HAVE HER **HEART** FOR ANYTHING.

SAY YOUR **PRAYERS, MISS EYRE,** WHEN YOU ARE BY **YOURSELF;** FOR IF YOU DON'T **REPENT,** SOMETHING **BAD** MIGHT BE PERMITTED TO COME DOWN THE **CHIMNEY** AND **FETCH YOU AWAY.**

UNJUST! - UNJUST!

HUH?!?

SHREEIK!!!

TAKE ME **OUT!**

LET ME GO INTO THE **NURSERY!**

BANG! BANG! BANG!

WELL, WHO **AM I?**

MR. **LLOYD...**

~ CHAPTER III ~

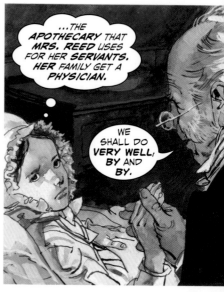

...THE **APOTHECARY** THAT **MRS. REED** USES FOR HER **SERVANTS.** HER FAMILY GET A **PHYSICIAN.**

WE SHALL DO **VERY WELL,** BY AND BY.

WOULD YOU LIKE TO **DRINK,** OR COULD YOU **EAT** ANYTHING?

NO, THANK YOU, BESSIE. WHAT IS THE **MATTER** WITH ME? AM I **ILL?**

YOU FELL **SICK,** I SUPPOSE, IN THE **RED-ROOM** WITH **CRYING;** YOU'LL BE **BETTER** SOON, NO **DOUBT.** YOU MAY **CALL** ME IF YOU WANT ANYTHING IN THE **NIGHT.** I WILL BE SLEEPING **NEXT DOOR.**

NEXT MORNING...

WELL, YOU HAVE BEEN **CRYING,** MISS **JANE EYRE:** CAN YOU TELL ME WHAT **ABOUT?** HAVE YOU ANY **PAIN?**

NO, SIR.

I DARESAY SHE IS **CRYING** BECAUSE SHE COULD NOT GO OUT WITH **MISSIS** IN THE **CARRIAGE.**

SURELY **NOT!** WHY, SHE IS TOO **OLD** FOR SUCH **PETTISHNESS.**

I NEVER **CRIED** FOR SUCH A THING IN MY **LIFE**. I **HATE** GOING OUT IN THE **CARRIAGE**. I **CRY** BECAUSE I AM **MISERABLE**.

OH **FIE**, MISS!

WHAT MADE YOU **ILL** YESTERDAY?

SHE HAD A **FALL**.

A **FALL**! THAT IS LIKE A **BABY** AGAIN!

CAN'T SHE MANAGE TO **WALK** AT **HER** AGE? SHE MUST BE **EIGHT** OR **NINE** YEARS OLD.

I WAS KNOCKED **DOWN**... BUT **THAT** DID NOT MAKE ME **ILL**.

THAT BELL IS FOR **YOU**, NURSE.

RING!!!

YOU CAN GO DOWN FOR YOUR **DINNER** NOW. I WILL GIVE **MISS JANE** A **LECTURE** UNTIL YOU COME **BACK**.

THE **FALL** DID NOT MAKE YOU ILL. WHAT **DID**, THEN?

I WAS **SHUT UP** IN A **ROOM** WHERE THERE IS A **GHOST**, TILL AFTER **DARK**.

GHOST! WHAT? YOU **ARE** A **BABY** AFTER **ALL**! YOU ARE **AFRAID** OF **GHOSTS**?

OF **MR. REED'S** GHOST I **AM**.

HE **DIED** IN THAT ROOM AND WAS **LAID OUT** THERE.

NO-ONE GOES INTO IT AT **NIGHT** IF THEY CAN **HELP** IT; AND IT WAS **CRUEL** TO SHUT ME UP **ALONE** WITHOUT A **CANDLE** --

-- SO **CRUEL** I THINK I SHALL **NEVER FORGET** IT.

15

NONSENSE! AND IS IT *THAT* MAKES YOU SO MISERABLE *NOW*? ARE YOU *AFRAID* NOW IN *DAYLIGHT*?

NO, BUT *NIGHT* WILL COME *AGAIN* BEFORE LONG -

AND *BESIDES* -

I AM *UNHAPPY*, *VERY* UNHAPPY, FOR *OTHER* THINGS.

WHAT OTHER THINGS?

I HAVE NO *MOTHER*, *BROTHERS* OR *SISTERS*.

YOU HAVE A KIND *AUNT* AND *COUSINS*...

BUT *JOHN REED* KNOCKED ME *DOWN* AND MY *AUNT* SHUT ME UP IN THE *RED-ROOM*.

HAVE YOU ANY RELATIONS *BESIDES* MRS. REED?

I DON'T *KNOW*. I *ASKED* AUNT REED ONCE, AND SHE SAID POSSIBLY I MIGHT HAVE SOME *POOR*, *LOW* RELATIONS CALLED *EYRE*, BUT SHE KNEW *NOTHING* ABOUT THEM.

IF YOU *HAD* SUCH, WOULD YOU LIKE TO GO TO *THEM*?

NO, I *NOT* LIKE TO BELONG TO *POOR* PEOPLE.

POVERTY TO ME WAS *SYNONYMOUS* WITH *DEGRADATION*.

WOULD YOU LIKE TO GO TO *SCHOOL*?

I SHOULD *INDEED* LIKE TO GO TO SCHOOL.

WELL, WELL; WHO KNOWS *WHAT* MAY *HAPPEN*?

THE *CHILD* OUGHT TO HAVE A *CHANGE* OF *AIR* AND *SCENE* - NERVES NOT IN A GOOD *STATE*.

THEY THINK I AM *ASLEEP*.

MISSIS WAS, SHE **DARED** SAY, **GLAD ENOUGH** TO GET **RID** OF SUCH A **TIRESOME, ILL-CONDITIONED** CHILD, WHO ALWAYS LOOKED AS IF SHE WERE **WATCHING** EVERYBODY AND **SCHEMING PLOTS** UNDERHAND.

HER **MOTHER** MARRIED THAT **POOR CLERGYMAN** AGAINST THE WISHES OF HER **FRIENDS**, WHO THOUGHT HIM **BENEATH** HER, AND OF HER **FATHER** MR. **REED** --

-- WHO **CUT HER OFF** WITHOUT A **SHILLING**.

THEN, BUT MARRIED A **YEAR**, THE **CLERGYMAN** CAUGHT THE **TYPHUS FEVER** WHILE VISITING AMONG THE **POOR** --

-- HER **MOTHER** THEN CAUGHT IT FROM **HIM** AND **BOTH** DIED WITHIN A **MONTH** OF EACH **OTHER**.

POOR MISS **JANE** IS TO BE PITIED **TOO**, ABBOTT.

YES, IF SHE WERE A **NICE, PRETTY** CHILD; BUT ONE REALLY **CANNOT** CARE FOR SUCH A LITTLE **TOAD** AS THAT.

~ CHAPTER IV ~

SOME WEEKS LATER...

18

MY **UNCLE REED** IS IN **HEAVEN**, AND CAN **SEE** ALL YOU **DO** AND **THINK**; AND SO CAN **PAPA** AND **MAMMA**:

THEY **KNOW** HOW YOU **SHUT ME UP** ALL DAY LONG AND WISH ME **DEAD**.

WHAT?

SLAP!

NOVEMBER, DECEMBER AND HALF OF *JANUARY* PASSED AWAY. *CHRISTMAS* AND THE *NEW YEAR* WERE CELEBRATED AT GATESHEAD WITH THE USUAL *FESTIVE CHEER*; *PRESENTS* HAD BEEN INTERCHANGED, *DINNERS* AND *EVENING PARTIES* GIVEN.

FROM *EVERY ENJOYMENT*, I WAS *EXCLUDED*.

ON THE *FIFTEENTH OF JANUARY*, I WAS CALLED TO *MRS. REED*...

THIS IS THE **LITTLE GIRL** RESPECTING WHOM I **APPLIED** TO YOU.

HER **SIZE** IS **SMALL**. WHAT IS HER **AGE**?

TEN YEARS.

YOUR **NAME**, LITTLE GIRL?

JANE EYRE, SIR.

ARE YOU A **GOOD** CHILD?

PERHAPS THE **LESS** SAID ON THAT SUBJECT THE **BETTER**, MR. BROCKLEHURST.

DO YOU **KNOW** WHERE THE **WICKED** GO AFTER **DEATH?**

AND WHAT **IS** HELL?

THEY GO TO **HELL.**

A **PIT** FULL OF **FIRE.**

WHAT MUST YOU DO TO **AVOID** IT?

I MUST KEEP IN **GOOD HEALTH,** AND **NOT** DIE.

CHILDREN **YOUNGER** THAN **YOU** DIE **DAILY.**

MR. **BROCKLEHURST,** **THIS** LITTLE GIRL IS NOT **QUITE** THE **CHARACTER** AND **DISPOSITION** I COULD **WISH;** SHE MUST BE **WATCHED CLOSELY** TO GUARD AGAINST HER **WORST FAULT** - A **TENDENCY** TO **DECEIT.**
I WISH HER TO BE MADE **USEFUL,** KEPT **HUMBLE,** BROUGHT UP IN A **MANNER** SUITING HER **PROSPECTS,** AND TO SPEND **ALL VACATIONS** AT **LOWOOD SCHOOL.**

HUMILITY IS A **CHRISTIAN GRACE.**

I **MORTIFY** PUPILS AT LOWOOD AGAINST THE **WORLDLY SENTIMENT** OF **PRIDE.**

AFTER **VISITING** MY SCHOOL, MY **SECOND** DAUGHTER, **AUGUSTA,** EXCLAIMED:

HOW **QUIET** AND **PLAIN** THE GIRLS LOOK - LIKE **POOR PEOPLE'S** CHILDREN.

THEY LOOKED AT MY **DRESS** AND **MAMMA'S** AS IF THEY HAD **NEVER** SEEN A **SILK GOWN** BEFORE.

HAD I SOUGHT **ALL ENGLAND** OVER, I COULD **SCARCELY** HAVE FOUND A SYSTEM MORE **EXACTLY** FITTING A **CHILD** LIKE **JANE EYRE.**

NO **DOUBT,** NO **DOUBT,** MADAM.

GO OUT OF THE **ROOM.** RETURN TO THE **NURSERY.**

IF I WERE **DECEITFUL,** I WOULD SAY I **LOVED** YOU.

BUT I DECLARE I *DO NOT* LOVE YOU.

I AM *GLAD* YOU ARE *NO RELATION* OF MINE.

I'LL *NEVER* CALL YOU *AUNT* AGAIN AS *LONG AS I LIVE.*

THE VERY *THOUGHT* OF YOU MAKES ME *SICK.*

HOW *DARE* YOU, *JANE EYRE!*

HOW *DARE I?* BECAUSE IT IS THE *TRUTH. YOU* HAVE *NO PITY.*

I SHALL *REMEMBER* YOUR *PUNISHMENT* OF ME WHEN YOUR *WICKED BOY* KNOCKED ME *DOWN* FOR *NOTHING.*

PEOPLE THINK YOU *GOOD,* BUT YOU ARE *BAD.*

YOU ARE *DECEITFUL.*

JANE, WHAT IS THE *MATTER* WITH YOU? WOULD YOU LIKE SOME *WATER?*

NO, MRS. REED.

I *ASSURE* YOU, I DESIRE TO BE YOUR *FRIEND.*

NOT *YOU.* YOU TOLD *MR. BROCKLEHURST* I HAD A *BAD CHARACTER,* A *DECEITFUL DISPOSITION.* I'LL LET *EVERYBODY* AT *LOWOOD* KNOW WHAT YOU *ARE* AND WHAT YOU HAVE *DONE.*

JANE, YOU DON'T *UNDERSTAND* THESE THINGS.

CHILDREN MUST BE *CORRECTED* FOR THEIR *FAULTS.*

DECEIT IS NOT MY *FAULT.*

BUT YOU ARE *PASSIONATE. THAT* YOU MUST *ALLOW.*

NOW *RETURN* TO THE *NURSERY* - THERE'S A DEAR. *LIE DOWN* A LITTLE.

I AM *NOT* YOUR *DEAR.* I *CANNOT* LIE DOWN.

SEND ME TO *SCHOOL* SOON, MRS. REED, FOR I *HATE* TO *LIVE* HERE.

21

I WILL **INDEED** SEND HER TO **SCHOOL** SOON.

I STOOD THERE **ALONE, WINNER** OF THE **FIELD,** AND ENJOYED MY **CONQUEROR'S SOLITUDE.**

BUT THIS FIERCE PLEASURE **SUBSIDED** IN ME AS FAST AS DID MY **PULSES.**

A CHILD CANNOT **QUARREL** WITH ITS **ELDERS** WITHOUT EXPERIENCING THE **PANG** OF **REMORSE.**

HALF AN HOUR'S **REFLECTION** SHOWED ME THE **MADNESS** OF MY **CONDUCT.**

BESSIE **COMFORTED ME** THAT AFTERNOON, TELLING ME HER MOST ENCHANTING **STORIES** AND SINGING HER **SWEETEST SONGS.**

YOU ARE A **STRANGE** CHILD, JANE... A LITTLE **ROVING, SOLITARY** THING.

WON'T YOU BE **SORRY** TO LEAVE POOR **BESSIE?**

WHAT DOES **BESSIE** CARE? SHE IS ALWAYS **SCOLDING** ME.

BECAUSE YOU'RE SUCH A **QUEER, FRIGHTENED, SHY** LITTLE THING YOU SHOULD BE **BOLDER.**

WHAT? TO GET MORE **KNOCKS?**

NONSENSE!

EVEN FOR **ME,** LIFE HAD ITS **GLEAMS** OF **SUNSHINE.**

FIVE O'CLOCK HAD BARELY **STRUCK** ON THE NINETEENTH OF JANUARY WHEN **BESSIE** BROUGHT A CANDLE INTO MY CLOSET, AND FOUND ME **ALREADY DRESSING** BY THE LIGHT OF A JUST-SETTING **HALF-MOON**.

~ CHAPTER V ~

WILL YOU GO IN AND BID MISSIS GOODBYE?

NO, BESSIE: SHE CAME TO MY **CRIB** LAST NIGHT AND SAID I NEED NOT **DISTURB** HER IN THE MORNING, NOR MY **COUSINS** EITHER;

AND SHE TOLD ME TO SAY SHE HAD BEEN MY **BEST FRIEND**.

WHAT DID **YOU** SAY, MISS?

NOTHING. I COVERED MY **FACE** WITH THE **BED-CLOTHES** AND TURNED FROM **HER** TO THE **WALL**.

THAT WAS **WRONG**, MISS **JANE**.

IT WAS QUITE **RIGHT**, BESSIE. YOUR **MISSIS** HAS NOT BEEN MY **FRIEND**. SHE HAS BEEN MY **FOE**.

GOODBYE TO GATESHEAD!

THE DAY SEEMED TO ME OF **PRETERNATURAL LENGTH**, AND WE **APPEARED** TO TRAVEL OVER **HUNDREDS OF MILES OF ROAD**.

I HAD **AT LAST** DROPPED **ASLEEP** WHEN THE SUDDEN **CESSATION** OF MOTION AWOKE ME.

IS THERE A **LITTLE GIRL** HERE CALLED JANE EYRE?

YES

THE **CHILD** IS VERY **YOUNG** TO BE SENT **ALONE.** SHE HAD BETTER BE **PUT TO BED** SOON; SHE LOOKS **TIRED.**

ARE YOU **TIRED?**

A **LITTLE,** MA'AM

AND **HUNGRY TOO,** NO DOUBT.

LET HER HAVE SOME **SUPPER** BEFORE SHE GOES TO **BED,** MISS **MILLER.**

I WAS CHANGED INTO MY UNIFORM AND TAKEN INTO A WIDE, LONG ROOM.

MONITORS, COLLECT THE **LESSON-BOOKS** AND **PUT THEM AWAY!**

MONITORS, FETCH THE **SUPPER-TRAYS!**

24

THE **MEAL** OVER, **PRAYERS** WERE READ BY **MISS MILLER**, AND THE CLASS **FILED OFF**, TWO AND TWO, UPSTAIRS. EACH **BED** WAS FILLED WITH **TWO OCCUPANTS**, AND **TO-NIGHT** I WAS TO BE **MISS MILLER'S** BED-FELLOW.

THE **NIGHT** PASSED **RAPIDLY** AND WE WERE **AWOKEN** BY A **LOUD BELL**.

Disgusting! The porridge is **burnt** again!

SILENCE!

WHY IS EVERYONE **STANDING?** I HAD HEARD NO **ORDER** GIVEN.

IT WAS THE **SUPERINTENDENT** OF **LOWOOD**, MISS TEMPLE.

YOU HAD THIS **MORNING** A **BREAKFAST** YOU COULD NOT **EAT**. YOU MUST BE **HUNGRY**.

I HAVE **ORDERED** THAT A **LUNCH** OF **BREAD AND CHEESE** BE SERVED TO **ALL**.

BREAD AND **CHEESE!** WE ARE HAVING **LUNCH!**

"LOWOOD INSTITUTION ... REBUILT BY NAOMI BROCKLEHURST OF BROCKLEHURST HALL ...'LET YOUR LIGHT SO SHINE BEFORE MEN THAT THEY MAY SEE YOUR GOOD WORKS AND GLORIFY YOUR FATHER WHICH IS IN HEAVEN.' - ST. MATTHEW, VERSE 16."

COUGH!

IS YOUR BOOK INTERESTING?

I LIKE IT.

WHAT IS IT ABOUT?

YOU MAY LOOK AT IT.

THIS LOOKS DULL. NOTHING ABOUT FAIRIES OR GENII.

CAN YOU TELL ME, WHAT IS LOWOOD INSTITUTION?

THIS HOUSE WHERE YOU ARE COME TO LIVE. IT IS PARTLY A CHARITY SCHOOL FOR EDUCATING ORPHANS.

CHARITY? DO WE PAY NO MONEY?

WE PAY, OR OUR FRIENDS PAY, FIFTEEN POUNDS A YEAR.

THEN WHY DO THEY CALL US CHARITY CHILDREN?

BECAUSE FIFTEEN POUNDS IS NOT ENOUGH FOR BOARD AND TEACHING.

THE DEFICIENCY IS SUPPLIED BY BENEVOLENT-MINDED LADIES AND GENTLEMEN.

IS HE A **GOOD** MAN, MR. **BROCKLEHURST?**

HE IS A **CLERGYMAN**, AND IS SAID TO DO A **GREAT DEAL OF GOOD.**

BUT **MISS TEMPLE** IS THE **BEST** - ISN'T SHE?

SHE IS **ABOVE** THE **REST.**

HAVE YOU BEEN **LONG** HERE?

TWO YEARS.

ARE YOU **HAPPY** HERE?

YOU ASK **RATHER TOO MANY QUESTIONS.** I HAVE GIVEN YOU **ANSWERS ENOUGH** FOR THE PRESENT. **NOW** I WANT TO **READ.**

~ CHAPTER VI ~

THE NEXT **MORNING** WE COULD NOT **WASH** AS THE **WATER** IN THE **PITCHERS** WAS **FROZEN.** LATER THAT **AFTERNOON,** MY **NEW** FRIEND BECAME THE **SUBJECT** OF **ATTENTION...**

YOU **DIRTY, DISAGREEABLE** GIRL! YOU HAVE **NEVER CLEANED** YOUR **NAILS** THIS MORNING!

WHY DOES SHE NOT **EXPLAIN** THAT SHE COULD NEITHER **CLEAN** HER **NAILS** NOR **WASH** HER **FACE,** AS THE **WATER** WAS **FROZEN?**

HARDENED GIRL! NOTHING CAN CORRECT YOU OF YOUR **SLATTERNLY HABITS:**

CARRY THE **ROD AWAY.**

THAT EVENING...

YOU MUST WISH TO **LEAVE** LOWOOD.

NO, WHY **SHOULD I?** I WAS **SENT HERE** TO GET AN **EDUCATION.**

BUT THAT **TEACHER,** MISS **SCATCHERD,** IS SO **CRUEL** TO YOU!

CRUEL? NOT AT **ALL.** SHE IS **SEVERE.** SHE DISLIKES MY **FAULTS.**

IF **I** WERE IN **YOUR** PLACE I SHOULD **DISLIKE** HER. IF SHE **STRUCK** ME WITH THAT **ROD,** I SHOULD **BREAK IT** UNDER HER **NOSE.**

IF YOU **DID,** MR. **BROCKLEHURST** WOULD **EXPEL** YOU.

IT IS FAR **BETTER** TO ENDURE **PATIENTLY** A **SMART** WHICH **NOBODY** FEELS BUT **YOURSELF.**

IF PEOPLE WERE ALWAYS *KIND* AND *OBEDIENT* TO THOSE WHO ARE *CRUEL* AND *UNJUST*, THE *WICKED* PEOPLE WOULD HAVE IT *ALL THEIR OWN WAY*;

THEY WOULD NEVER FEEL *AFRAID*, AND THEY WOULD NEVER *ALTER*.

WHEN WE ARE *STRUCK* AT WITHOUT A *REASON*, WE SHOULD *STRIKE BACK* AGAIN VERY *HARD* - SO HARD AS TO *TEACH* THE PERSON WHO *STRUCK* US NEVER TO DO IT *AGAIN*.

IT IS AS *NATURAL* AS *LOVING* THOSE WHO SHOW US *AFFECTION*.

HEATHENS AND SAVAGE TRIBES HOLD THAT DOCTRINE. BUT *CIVILISED* NATIONS *DISOWN* IT.

IT IS NOT *VIOLENCE* THAT BEST OVERCOMES *HATE*, NOR *VENGEANCE* THAT MOST CERTAINLY HEALS *INJURY* --

-- *READ* THE *NEW TESTAMENT* AND OBSERVE HOW *CHRIST* ACTS. MAKE HIS *WORD* YOUR *RULE* AND HIS *CONDUCT* YOUR *EXAMPLE*.

WHAT DOES HE *SAY*?

LOVE YOUR *ENEMIES*. *BLESS* THEM THAT *CURSE* YOU. DO *GOOD* TO THEM THAT *HATE* AND *USE* YOU.

THEN I SHOULD *LOVE* MRS. *REED*, WHICH I CANNOT DO. I SHOULD *BLESS* HER SON *JOHN*, WHICH IS *IMPOSSIBLE*.

I PROCEEDED TO *POUR OUT* THE TALE OF MY *SUFFERINGS*, SPEAKING AS I *FELT*, WITHOUT *RESERVE* OR SOFTENING. *HELEN* HEARD ME *PATIENTLY* TO THE *END*.

MRS. **REED** WAS **UNKIND** TO YOU BECAUSE SHE **DISLIKES** YOUR **CAST** OF **CHARACTER**, AS MISS SCATCHERD DOES MINE.

BUT HOW **MINUTELY** YOU REMEMBER EVERYTHING!

WOULD YOU NOT BE **HAPPIER** IF YOU TRIED TO **FORGET** HER SEVERITY AND YOUR **PASSIONATE EMOTIONS?**

LIFE APPEARS TO **ME** TOO **SHORT** TO BE SPENT IN NURSING **ANIMOSITY**. WE ARE ALL **BURDENED** WITH **FAULTS**.

SOON WE SHALL **PUT OFF** OUR **CORRUPTIBLE** BODIES AND ONLY THE **SPARK** OF OUR **SPIRIT** WILL **REMAIN**.

I CAN SINCERELY **FORGIVE** THE **CRIMINAL** WHILE I **ABHOR** THE **CRIME**.

REVENGE NEVER **WORRIES** MY **HEART** AND **DEGRADATION** NEVER TOO DEEPLY **DISGUSTS** ME. I LIVE IN **CALM**, LOOKING TO THE **END**.

~ CHAPTER VII ~

MY **FIRST QUARTER** AT **LOWOOD** SEEMED AN **AGE**, AND NOT THE **GOLDEN AGE** EITHER ...

JANUARY...

...WITH THE **KEEN APPETITES** OF GROWING **CHILDREN**, WE WERE FED SCARCELY **SUFFICIENT** TO KEEP **ALIVE** A **DELICATE INVALID**...

...WHENEVER THE **FAMISHED GREAT GIRLS** HAD AN **OPPORTUNITY**, THEY WOULD **COAX** OR **MENACE** THE **LITTLE ONES** OUT OF **THEIR** PORTION...

...ONE **AFTERNOON** (I HAD BEEN **THREE WEEKS** AT **LOWOOD**), THE **MOMENT** I HAD **DREADED** ARRIVED...

...I WAS **SURE** MR. **BROCKLEHURST** WAS ABOUT TO **FULFILL** HIS **PROMISE** TO MRS. **REED** TO DISCLOSE MY **VICIOUS NATURE** TO MISS **TEMPLE** AND THE **TEACHERS**.

...AND SHE IS **NOT**, ON **ANY ACCOUNT**, TO GIVE OUT **MORE** THAN **ONE DARNING NEEDLE** AT A **TIME** TO EACH PUPIL.

A **LUNCH** OF **BREAD** AND **CHEESE** HAS **TWICE** BEEN SERVED DURING THE PAST **FORTNIGHT**.

NO SUCH **MEAL** AS **LUNCH** IS **ALLOWED**. WHO **INTRODUCED** THIS **INNOVATION**? AND BY WHAT **AUTHORITY**?

I MUST BE **RESPONSIBLE**, SIR. THE **BREAKFAST** WAS SO **ILL-PREPARED** THAT THEY COULD NOT **POSSIBLY** EAT IT; AND I **DARED** NOT ALLOW THEM TO REMAIN **FASTING** TILL **DINNER-TIME**.

MADAM, MY PLAN IS NOT TO **ACCUSTOM** THEM TO HABITS OF **LUXURY** AND **INDULGENCE**, BUT TO RENDER THEM **HARDY, PATIENT, SELF-DENYING.**

A **JUDICIOUS INSTRUCTOR** WOULD TAKE THE **OPPORTUNITY** OF REFERRING TO THE **SUFFERINGS** OF THE **PRIMITIVE CHRISTIANS**; THAT **MAN** SHALL NOT **LIVE** BY **BREAD** ALONE.

WHEN YOU PUT **BREAD** AND **CHEESE** INSTEAD OF **BURNT PORRIDGE** INTO CHILDREN'S MOUTHS, YOU MAY **FEED** THEIR **VILE BODIES**, BUT HOW YOU **STARVE** THEIR **IMMORTAL SOULS!**

...MISS **TEMPLE**, WHAT IS THAT **GIRL** WITH **CURLED HAIR**? RED HAIR, MA'AM, **CURLED** ALL OVER?

IT IS **JULIA SEVERN**. HER HAIR CURLS **NATURALLY.**

I **DESIRE** THE **HAIR** TO BE **ARRANGED CLOSELY, MODESTLY, PLAINLY.**

TELL ALL THE **FIRST FORM** TO DIRECT THEIR **FACES** TO THE **WALL.**

ALL THOSE **TOP-KNOTS** MUST BE **CUT OFF.**

BUT **SIR** -

MADAM, MY **MISSION** IS TO **MORTIFY** THE **LUSTS** OF THE **FLESH**, TO **TEACH** THESE GIRLS TO **CLOTHE** THEMSELVES WITH **SHAME-FACEDNESS**, AND **SOBRIETY**,

NOT WITH **BRAIDED HAIR** AND **COSTLY APPAREL.**

MRS. **BROCKLEHURST**, WELCOME. PLEASE, DO SIT **DOWN**, YOU AND YOUR **DAUGHTERS.**

CRASH!

31

A CARELESS GIRL!

IT IS THE **NEW PUPIL**, I PERCEIVE. I HAVE A **WORD** TO SAY RESPECTING **HER**.

LET THE CHILD WHO BROKE HER **SLATE** COME FORWARD.

Don't be *afraid*, Jane, I saw it was an *accident*; you shall *not* be punished.

ANOTHER *MINUTE*, AND SHE WILL *DESPISE* ME FOR A *HYPOCRITE*.

LADIES, MISS **TEMPLE**, TEACHERS AND **CHILDREN**, YOU ALL SEE THIS **GIRL**?

OBSERVE SHE POSSESSES THE **ORDINARY** FORM OF **CHILDHOOD** GRACIOUSLY GIVEN TO HER BY **GOD**.

WHO WOULD **THINK** THAT THE **EVIL ONE** HAD **ALREADY** FOUND A **SERVANT** AND **AGENT** IN HER?

How shocking!

BE ON **GUARD** AGAINST HER. **AVOID** HER **COMPANY**. TEACHERS, SCRUTINISE HER **ACTIONS**, PUNISH HER **BODY** TO SAVE HER **SOUL**. THIS GIRL IS –

A LIAR!

HER **PIOUS**, CHARITABLE **BENEFACTRESS** TOLD ME THIS **UNHAPPY ORPHAN** REPAID HER WITH **INGRATITUDE**. LET HER STAND HALF AN HOUR **LONGER** ON THAT **STOOL**, AND LET **NO ONE** SPEAK TO HER DURING THE **REMAINDER** OF THE **DAY**.

THERE WAS I, THEN, *EXPOSED* TO GENERAL VIEW ON A PEDESTAL OF *INFAMY*. WHAT MY *SENSATIONS* WERE, *NO LANGUAGE* CAN DESCRIBE. A GIRL PASSED ME AND LIFTED HER *EYES*.

WHAT AN **EXTRAORDINARY** SENSATION THAT RAY SENT THROUGH ME.

MISS **SCATCHERD** CONDEMNED *HELEN BURNS* TO A DINNER OF **BREAD AND WATER** BECAUSE SHE **BLOTTED** A PAGE WITH **INK**.

UNTIDY.

SUCH **SPOTS** ARE ON THE **DISC** OF THE **CLEAREST PLANET**; AND EYES LIKE MISS **SCATCHERD'S** CAN ONLY SEE THOSE **MINUTE DEFECTS**, AND ARE **BLIND** TO THE **FULL BRIGHTNESS** OF THE **ORB**.

~ CHAPTER VIII ~

ERE THE HALF HOUR ENDED, FIVE O'CLOCK STRUCK; SCHOOL WAS DISMISSED, AND ALL WERE GONE INTO THE REFECTORY FOR TEA.

LEFT TO *MYSELF*, I WEPT; AND MY TEARS WATERED THE *BOARDS*.

COME, EAT SOMETHING.

HELEN, WHY DO YOU *STAY* WITH A GIRL WHOM *EVERYONE* BELIEVES TO BE A *LIAR?*

EVERYBODY, JANE? ONLY *EIGHTY PEOPLE* HAVE HEARD YOU CALLED SO. THE WORLD CONTAINS *HUNDREDS* OF *MILLIONS*.

THE EIGHTY I KNOW *DESPISE* ME.

JANE, PROBABLY NOT *ONE* IN THE SCHOOL *DESPISES* OR *DISLIKES* YOU. MR. *BROCKLEHURST* IS NOT A *GOD*. NOR IS HE EVEN *LIKED* HERE.

IF OTHERS DON'T *LOVE ME*, I WOULD RATHER *DIE* THAN *LIVE*. I CANNOT *BEAR* TO BE SOLITARY AND *HATED*, HELEN.

HUSH, JANE! YOU THINK *TOO MUCH* OF THE *LOVE OF HUMAN BEINGS*. BESIDES THIS *EARTH* AND THE RACE OF *MEN*, THERE IS AN *INVISIBLE WORLD* AND A *KINGDOM OF SPIRITS*.

ANGELS SEE OUR *TORTURES* AND *RECOGNISE* OUR *INNOCENCE* --

≶ COUGH ≶

I *CAME* ON PURPOSE TO *INVITE YOU* TO MY *ROOM*, JANE EYRE. AS HELEN BURNS IS WITH YOU, SHE MAY COME *TOO*.

WE SHALL *THINK* YOU WHAT YOU *PROVE YOURSELF* TO BE, MY *CHILD*. CONTINUE TO ACT AS A *GOOD GIRL*, AND YOU WILL *SATISFY US*.

NOW *TELL ME*, WHO IS THE *LADY* WHOM MR. *BROCKLEHURST* CALLED YOUR *BENEFACTRESS?*

MRS. *REED*, MY *UNCLE'S* WIFE.

MY *UNCLE* IS *DEAD*, AND HE LEFT ME TO HER *CARE*.

DID **MRS. REED** NOT **ADOPT** YOU OF HER **OWN** ACCORD?

NO, MA'AM. THE **SERVANTS** SAID THAT MY **UNCLE** GOT HER TO **PROMISE** BEFORE HE **DIED** THAT SHE WOULD ALWAYS **KEEP** ME.

THEN I TOLD HER THE STORY OF MY **SAD** CHILDHOOD, OF THE **RED-ROOM** AND MY **FIT** - IN THE COURSE OF WHICH I MENTIONED **MR. LLOYD.**

I HAVE **HEARD** SOMETHING OF MR. LLOYD AND SHALL **WRITE** TO HIM. IF HIS **REPLY** AGREES WITH YOUR STATEMENT, YOU SHALL BE **PUBLICLY CLEARED** FROM EVERY **IMPUTATION.**

TO ME, **JANE,** YOU ARE **CLEAR** NOW.

HOW **ARE** YOU TO-NIGHT, **HELEN?** HAVE YOU **COUGHED** MUCH TODAY?

NOT **QUITE** SO MUCH, I THINK, MA'AM.

MISS TEMPLE SHOWED **GENUINE** CONCERN FOR US. AFTER SHE GAVE US A **SUPPER TREAT** OF **TEA, TOAST** AND **CAKE,** THE BELL ANNOUNCED OUR **BEDTIME** AND WE LEFT HER WITH A **TEAR** ON HER **CHEEK.**

ABOUT A **WEEK LATER** AT A **SCHOOL ASSEMBLY...**

AN **ENQUIRY** WAS MADE INTO THE **CHARGES** AGAINST **JANE EYRE,** AND I AM **MOST HAPPY** TO **PRONOUNCE** THAT SHE HAS BEEN **CLEARED** OF **EVERY ACCUSATION** MADE **AGAINST** HER.

~ CHAPTER IX ~

THE **HARDSHIPS** OF LOWOOD **LESSENED** AS **SPRING** DREW ON. MY WRETCHED **FEET, FLAYED** AND **SWOLLEN** TO **LAMENESS** BY THE **SHARP AIR** OF **JANUARY,** BEGAN TO **HEAL.**

LOWOOD SHOOK **LOOSE** ITS **TRESSES.** IT BECAME ALL **FLOWERY** WITH **SNOW-DROPS, CROCUSES, PURPLE AURICULAS, LILIES, ROSES, WILD PRIMROSES** AND **GOLDEN-EYED PANSIES.**

ITS GREAT **ELM, ASH,** AND **OAK SKELETONS** WERE **RESTORED** TO **MAJESTIC LIFE.**

BUT THAT **FOREST-DELL**, WHERE **LOWOOD** LAY, WAS THE **CRADLE** OF **FOG** AND **FOG-BRED PESTILENCE**;

WHICH, **QUICKENING** WITH THE QUICKENING **SPRING**, BREATHED **TYPHUS** INTO THE **ORPHAN ASYLUM**.

FORTY-FIVE OUT OF THE **EIGHTY** GIRLS LAY **ILL**.

CLASSES WERE **BROKEN UP** AND **RULES** WERE **RELAXED**. MISS **TEMPLE'S** WHOLE **ATTENTION** WAS ABSORBED BY THE **PATIENTS** AND SHE **LIVED** IN THE **SICK ROOM**.

MANY GIRLS, ALREADY SMITTEN, WENT **HOME** ONLY TO **DIE**. SOME **DIED** AT THE **SCHOOL**, AND WERE BURIED **QUIETLY** AND **QUICKLY**, THE NATURE OF THE **MALADY** FORBIDDING **DELAY**.

ENQUIRIES WERE MADE INTO THE **SCANDAL**...

SEMI-STARVATION AND NEGLECTED **COLDS** HAVE **PREDISPOSED** MOST OF THE **PUPILS** TO INFECTION.

NOT TO **MENTION** THEIR **THIN CLOTHING**, AND **WRETCHED ACCOMMO-DATION**.

AND THE **FETID WATER** IN THE **COOKING POTS**.

WERE THEY FED AT **ALL**, MR. **BROCKLEHURST**? I **UNDERSTAND** THAT YOU **BANNED** LUNCH.

HELEN WAS **ILL** AT PRESENT; FOR SOME WEEKS SHE HAD BEEN REMOVED FROM SIGHT. FINALLY HER **NURSE** TOLD ME **HELEN'S** BED WAS IN MISS **TEMPLE'S** ROOM, AS SHE HAD **CONSUMPTION**, NOT **TYPHUS**. SHE TOLD ME THAT I COULD **NOT SEE HER**, BUT I **CREPT** INTO HER ROOM AFTER ELEVEN.

Helen, are you awake?

WHY ARE YOU **COME** HERE, JANE? IT IS PAST **ELEVEN** O'CLOCK.

I CAME TO SEE **YOU**, HELEN. I HEARD YOU WERE VERY **ILL** AND I **COULD NOT SLEEP** TILL I HAD **SPOKEN** TO YOU.

YOU CAME TO BID ME **GOODBYE**, THEN. YOU ARE **JUST IN TIME**, PROBABLY.

ARE YOU **GOING HOME**, HELEN?

YES, TO MY **LAST** HOME.

NO, **NO**, HELEN!

≲COUGH≲

≲COUGH!≲

≲COUGH!!≲

JANE, YOUR LITTLE **FEET** ARE **BARE**. **LIE DOWN** AND **COVER** YOURSELF WITH MY **QUILT**.

I AM VERY **HAPPY**, JANE, AND WHEN YOU HEAR THAT I AM **DEAD**, YOU MUST BE SURE AND **NOT GRIEVE**. THERE IS **NOTHING** TO GRIEVE **ABOUT**.

BY DYING **YOUNG**, I SHALL ESCAPE GREAT **SUFFERINGS**. I HAD NOT **QUALITIES** OR **TALENTS** TO MAKE MY WAY VERY **WELL** IN THE **WORLD**.

BUT WHERE ARE YOU **GOING TO**, HELEN?

I AM **GOING** TO GOD.

LATER I LEARNED THAT **MISS TEMPLE** HAD **FOUND ME** THE NEXT MORNING, MY **ARMS** ROUND HELEN'S **NECK**. I WAS **ASLEEP**, AND HELEN WAS - **DEAD**.

CHAPTER X

AFTER *TYPHUS* DIED AWAY, WEALTHY BENEVOLENT INDIVIDUALS INTRODUCED *IMPROVEMENTS* IN *DIET, CLOTHING* AND *BUILDINGS* AT LOWOOD SCHOOL; AND MANAGEMENT BY *COMMITTEE.* MR. BROCKLEHURST BECAME *TREASURER,* SUPERVISED BY GENTLEMEN OF RATHER MORE *ENLARGED* AND *SYMPATHETIC* MINDS.

I REMAINED AN *INMATE* OF ITS WALLS FOR *EIGHT YEARS. SIX* AS A *PUPIL,* AND *TWO* AS A *TEACHER.*

I WAS *HAPPY* AS A *TEACHER* AT LOWOOD, BUT MY *TRANQUILLITY* DEPARTED WITH *MISS TEMPLE.*

YOU ARE NO LONGER *MOTHER, GOVERNESS* AND *COMPANION* TO ME - BUT *MRS. NASMYTH,* WIFE OF A *CLERGYMAN.*

FARE YOU *WELL!*

FARE *YOU* WELL, DEAREST *JANE.*

I *TIRED* OF THE ROUTINE OF *EIGHT YEARS* IN *ONE AFTERNOON.* I DESIRED *LIBERTY;* FOR *LIBERTY* I UTTERED A *PRAYER;* IT SEEMED *SCATTERED* ON THE *WIND* THEN FAINTLY BLOWING; SO I ASKED FOR *CHANGE, STIMULUS.* EVEN *THAT* SEEMED SWEPT OFF INTO A *VAGUE SPACE...*

...THEN, *GRANT ME* AT *LEAST* A NEW *SERVITUDE!*

I PLACED AN *ADVERTISEMENT* FOR MY *SERVICES* IN THE *HERALD NEWSPAPER.*

I RECEIVED ONLY *ONE* RESPONSE TO MY ADVERTISEMENT, FROM A *MRS. FAIRFAX* IN *THORNFIELD.* I ACCEPTED THE POST OF *GOVERNESS* IN HER HOUSE...

... AND ON THE *MORNING* OF MY *DEPARTURE,* I RECEIVED A *VISITOR.*

WELL, WHO *IS* IT?

YOU'VE NOT *QUITE* FORGOTTEN ME, I THINK, MISS JANE?

BESSIE!

BESSIE!

BESSIE!

MY LITTLE **BOY** HERE IS CALLED **BOBBY,** AND I'VE A LITTLE **GIRL** THAT I'VE CHRISTENED **JANE.**

I'VE BEEN **MARRIED** NEARLY **FIVE YEARS** TO THE **COACHMAN.**

AND YOU DON'T LIVE IN **GATESHEAD?**

I LIVE AT THE **LODGE:** THE **OLD PORTER** HAS **LEFT.**

TELL ME **EVERYTHING,** BESSIE.

LAST **WINTER,** A YOUNG **LORD** FELL IN LOVE WITH **MISS GEORGIANA,** BUT HIS **RELATIONS** WERE **AGAINST** THE MATCH; **AND** - WHAT DO YOU **THINK?** - HE AND **MISS GEORGIANA** MADE IT UP TO **RUN AWAY.**

MISS **ELIZA** FOUND THEM **OUT** AND **STOPPED** IT. I **BELIEVE** SHE WAS **ENVIOUS.**

NOW **SHE** AND HER **SISTER** LEAD A **CAT** AND **DOG** LIFE TOGETHER; THEY ARE **ALWAYS QUARRELLING.**

JOHN REED IS **NOT** DOING SO **WELL** AS HIS **MAMA** COULD **WISH.** HE WENT TO **COLLEGE** TO STUDY THE **LAW:**

BUT HE IS **SUCH A DISSIPATED YOUNG MAN,** THEY WILL **NEVER** MAKE **MUCH** OF HIM, I THINK.

AND **MRS. REED?**

MISSIS **LOOKS** STOUT AND WELL ENOUGH, BUT SHE'S **NOT QUITE** EASY IN HER **MIND.**

MR. **JOHN'S** CONDUCT DOES **NOT** PLEASE HER - HE **SPENDS A DEAL** OF **MONEY.**

DID **SHE** SEND YOU HERE, **BESSIE?**

NO INDEED; BUT I HAVE **LONG WANTED** TO SEE YOU, AND WHEN I **HEARD** THAT YOU WERE GOING TO **ANOTHER PART** OF THE **COUNTRY,**

I THOUGHT I'D GET A **LOOK** AT YOU BEFORE YOU WERE **QUITE** OUT OF MY **REACH.**

I **ALSO** LEARNED THAT AN **UNCLE** HAD CALLED TO GATESHEAD SEVEN YEARS AGO ASKING ABOUT ME. HE WAS DISAPPOINTED NOT TO SEE ME, AND HE HAD TO **LEAVE** FOR **MADEIRA.**

I WAS COLLECTED FROM THE *GEORGE INN* AT *MILLCOTE* BY A *PLAIN SERVANT* IN A *PLAIN CARRIAGE.* *THORNFIELD* WAS A SHORT *SIX MILES* AWAY.

WILL YOU *WALK* THIS *WAY,* MA'AM?

~ CHAPTER XI ~

MRS. *FAIRFAX,* I SUPPOSE?

YES, YOU ARE *RIGHT: DO* SIT *DOWN.*

I *DARESAY* YOUR *HANDS* ARE ALMOST *NUMBED* WITH *COLD.*

-- *LEAH,* MAKE A LITTLE *HOT HEGUS* AND CUT A *SANDWICH* OR TWO.

DRAW *NEARER* TO THE *FIRE.*

SHE TREATS ME LIKE A *VISITOR.* THIS IS *NOT* LIKE WHAT I HAVE HEARD OF THE TREATMENT OF *GOVERNESSES.*

SHALL I HAVE THE PLEASURE OF SEEING MISS FAIRFAX *TO-NIGHT?*

WHAT DID YOU SAY MY *DEAR?* OH, YOU MEAN MISS *VARENS!*

THEN SHE IS NOT YOUR *DAUGHTER?*

NO - I HAVE *NO* FAMILY.

I AM *SO* GLAD YOU ARE COME; IT WILL BE QUITE *PLEASANT* LIVING HERE NOW WITH A *COMPANION.*

BUT I'LL NOT KEEP YOU SITTING UP *LATE* TO-NIGHT, IT IS ON THE *STROKE* OF *TWELVE* NOW.

I'VE HAD THE **ROOM** NEXT TO **MINE** PREPARED FOR YOU.

I THOUGHT YOU WOULD LIKE IT **BETTER** THAN ONE OF THE **LARGER** CHAMBERS: THEY ARE SO **DREARY** AND **SOLITARY**.

NEXT **MORNING...**

THORNFIELD IS A VERY **PRETTY** PLACE.

YES IT **IS**; BUT I FEAR IT WILL BE GETTING **OUT OF ORDER**, UNLESS **MR. ROCHESTER** SHOULD RESIDE HERE **PERMANENTLY**.

MR. **ROCHESTER!** WHO IS **HE?**

THE **OWNER** OF **THORNFIELD.** DID YOU NOT **KNOW** HE WAS CALLED **ROCHESTER?**

I THOUGHT **THORNFIELD** BELONGED TO **YOU.**

TO **ME?** BLESS **YOU**, CHILD, WHAT AN **IDEA!** I AM ONLY THE **HOUSEKEEPER** - THE **MANAGER**.

AND THE LITTLE **GIRL** - MY **PUPIL?**

SHE IS MR. **ROCHESTER'S WARD**.

SO MUCH THE **BETTER** - MY **POSITION** HERE IS ALL THE **FREER.**

HERE SHE **COMES**, WITH HER **"BONNE"** AS SHE CALLS HER **NURSE**.

GOOD **MORNING**, MISS **ADÈLE.** COME AND SPEAK TO THE **LADY** WHO IS TO **TEACH YOU.**

C'EST LA MA GOUVERANTE!

MAIS OUI, CERTAINEMENT.

ARE THEY **FOREIGNERS?**

THE **NURSE** IS A FOREIGNER AND **ADÈLE** WAS BORN ON THE **CONTINENT;** AND, I BELIEVE, NEVER **LEFT IT** TILL WITHIN **SIX MONTHS AGO.**

I DON'T **UNDERSTAND** HER, SHE MIXES **ENGLISH** SO WITH **FRENCH.**

I LIVED **LONG AGO** WITH **MAMA,** BUT SHE IS GONE TO THE **HOLY VIRGIN.**

MAMA USED TO TEACH ME TO **DANCE AND SING,** AND TO SAY **VERSES.** A GREAT MANY GENTLEMEN AND LADIES CAME TO SEE **MAMA.**

I USED TO **DANCE** BEFORE THEM, OR SIT ON THEIR **KNEES** AND SING TO THEM.

AFTER **BREAKFAST, ADÈLE** AND I WITHDREW TO THE **LIBRARY.**

I FOUND MY PUPIL SUFFICIENTLY **DOCILE,** THOUGH **DISINCLINED** TO **APPLY:** SHE HAD NOT BEEN USED TO **REGULAR OCCUPATION** OF **ANY KIND.**

WHEN THE MORNING HAD ADVANCED TO **NOON,** I ALLOWED HER TO RETURN TO HER **NURSE.**

LATER, MRS. **FAIRFAX** SHOWED ME AROUND THE **HOUSE.**

IN WHAT **ORDER** YOU KEEP THESE **ROOMS,** MRS. **FAIRFAX!**

WHY, THOUGH MR. **ROCHESTER'S** VISITS ARE **RARE,** THEY ARE ALWAYS **SUDDEN** AND **UNEXPECTED.**

DO YOU **LIKE** HIM?

OH **YES;** THE **FAMILY** HAVE ALWAYS BEEN **RESPECTED** HERE.

SOME OF THE **THIRD-STOREY ROOMS** WERE **INTERESTING** FROM THEIR AIR OF **ANTIQUITY;** GIVING THE ASPECT OF A **HOME OF THE PAST** - A **SHRINE OF MEMORY.**

IF THERE WERE A **GHOST** AT **THORNFIELD HALL,** THIS WOULD BE ITS **HAUNT.**

SO I **THINK.**

YOU **HAVE** NO **GHOST,** THEN?

NONE THAT **I** EVER HEARD OF.

I FOLLOWED STILL, UP A VERY NARROW STAIRCASE TO THE ATTICS, AND THENCE BY A LADDER AND THROUGH A TRAP-DOOR TO THE ROOF OF THE HALL.

I WAS NOW ON A LEVEL WITH THE CROW COLONY AND COULD SEE INTO THEIR NESTS.

I PROCEEDED TO DESCEND WHEN...

AH-HA-HA...

MRS. FAIRFAX! DID YOU HEAR THAT LOUD LAUGH? WHO IS IT?

SOME OF THE SERVANTS, VERY LIKELY.

PERHAPS GRACE POOLE.

TOO MUCH NOISE, GRACE. REMEMBER DIRECTIONS!

WHO IS GRACE POOLE?

SHE IS A PERSON WE HAVE TO SEW AND ASSIST LEAH IN HER HOUSEMAID'S WORK; NOT ALTOGETHER UNOBJECTIONABLE IN SOME POINTS, BUT SHE DOES WELL ENOUGH.

THREE MONTHS *LATER,* IN *JANUARY,* MRS. *FAIRFAX* HAD JUST WRITTEN A *LETTER* WHICH WAS WAITING TO BE *POSTED,* SO I VOLUNTEERED TO *CARRY IT* TO *HAY;* THE *DISTANCE,* TWO MILES, WOULD BE A PLEASANT WINTER AFTERNOON *WALK.*

~ CHAPTER XII ~

A *RUDE NOISE* BROKE: A *HORSE* WAS COMING...

ROWF! ROWF!

WHOO-OOSH!!

WHAT THE *DEUCE* IS *TO DO* NOW?

ROWF! ROWF!

DOWN, PILOT!

IF YOU ARE *HURT,* AND WANT *HELP,* SIR, I CAN *FETCH* SOMEONE EITHER FROM *THORNFIELD HALL* OR FROM *HAY.*

I HAVE NO **BROKEN BONES** - ONLY A **SPRAIN.**

WHERE DO YOU **COME FROM?**

FROM JUST **BELOW;** I WILL RUN OVER TO **HAY** FOR YOU WITH **PLEASURE** IF YOU **WISH** IT; INDEED I AM **GOING THERE** TO POST A **LETTER.**

I SHOULD THINK **YOU** OUGHT TO BE AT HOME **YOURSELF.**

DO YOU COME FROM THAT **HOUSE** WITH THE **BATTLEMENTS?**

YES, SIR. I AM THE **GOVERNESS.**

AH, THE **GOVERNESS** - DEUCE TAKE ME IF I HAD NOT **FORGOTTEN!** THE **GOVERNESS!**

EXCUSE ME - **NECESSITY** COMPELS ME TO MAKE YOU **USEFUL.**

HE LAID A **HEAVY HAND** ON MY **SHOULDER** AND **LIMPED** TO HIS **HORSE.**

THANK YOU. NOW **MAKE HASTE** WITH THE LETTER TO **HAY,** AND **RETURN** AS **FAST** AS YOU **CAN.**

A **TOUCH** OF A **SPURRED HEEL** MADE HIS HORSE FIRST **START** AND **REAR,** AND THEN **BOUND AWAY.**

LIKE **HEATH** THAT; IN THE **WILDERNESS,** THE **WILD WIND** WHIRLS **AWAY.**

IT WAS AN INCIDENT OF **NO MOMENT,** YET IT MARKED WITH CHANGE ONE **SINGLE HOUR** OF MONOTONOUS LIFE. MY HELP HAD BEEN **NEEDED** AND **CLAIMED.**

TRANSITORY THOUGH THE DEED WAS, IT WAS YET AN **ACTIVE** THING, AND I WAS **WEARY** OF AN EXISTENCE ALL **PASSIVE.**

I DID NOT LIKE **RE-ENTERING** THORNFIELD. TO PASS ITS **THRESHOLD** WAS TO RETURN TO **STAGNATION.**

LEAH, WHAT **DOG** IS THIS?

HE CAME WITH **MASTER** -

MR. ROCHESTER - HE IS JUST **ARRIVED.**

JOHN IS GONE FOR A **SURGEON,** FOR MASTER HAS HAD AN **ACCIDENT.** HIS **HORSE** SLIPPED ON SOME **ICE** IN HAY LANE.

ADÈLE WAS NOT EASY TO **TEACH** THE NEXT DAY; SHE COULD NOT **APPLY.** SHE KEPT **RUNNING** TO THE **DOOR** AND LOOKING TO SEE IF SHE COULD GET A **GLIMPSE** OF **MR. ROCHESTER.**

~ CHAPTER XIII ~

LATER IN THE **AFTERNOON,** MRS. **FAIRFAX** CAME IN.

MR. ROCHESTER WOULD BE **GLAD** IF **YOU** AND YOUR **PUPIL** WOULD TAKE **TEA** WITH HIM IN THE **DRAWING-ROOM** THIS EVENING.

WHAT **IS** HIS TEA-TIME?

AT **SIX O'CLOCK.** HE KEEPS **EARLY HOURS** IN THE **COUNTRY.**

N'EST-CE PAS, MONSIEUR, QU'IL Y A UN **CADEAU** POUR **MADEMOISELLE EYRE** DANS VOTRE **PETIT COFFRE?**

WHO TALKS OF **CADEAUX?** DID YOU EXPECT A **PRESENT,** MISS **EYRE?** ARE YOU **FOND** OF PRESENTS?

I HARDLY **KNOW,** SIR. I HAVE LITTLE **EXPERIENCE** OF THEM. THEY ARE **GENERALLY** THOUGHT **PLEASANT** THINGS.

GENERALLY **THOUGHT?** BUT WHAT DO **YOU** THINK?

A **PRESENT** HAS **MANY FACES** TO IT; AND ONE SHOULD CONSIDER **ALL,** BEFORE PRONOUNCING AN **OPINION** AS TO IT'S **NATURE.**

MISS **EYRE,** YOU ARE NOT SO **UNSOPHISTICATED** AS ADÈLE. SHE DEMANDS A "**CADEAU**" **CLAMOROUSLY,** THE **MOMENT** SHE **SEES** ME: **YOU** BEAT ABOUT THE **BUSH.**

BECAUSE I HAVE LESS **CONFIDENCE** IN MY **DESERTS** THAN ADÈLE HAS.

I AM A **STRANGER** AND HAVE DONE **NOTHING** TO ENTITLE ME TO AN **ACKNOWLEDGEMENT.**

OH, DON'T FALL BACK ON OVER-MODESTY!

I HAVE EXAMINED ADÈLE, AND FIND YOU HAVE TAKEN GREAT PAINS WITH HER. SHE HAS NO TALENTS, YET IN A SHORT TIME SHE HAS MADE MUCH IMPROVEMENT.

SIR, YOU HAVE NOW GIVEN ME MY "CADEAU"; I AM OBLIGED TO YOU: IT IS THE MEED TEACHERS MOST COVET - PRAISE OF THEIR PUPILS' PROGRESS.

HUMPH!

YOU HAVE BEEN RESIDENT IN MY HOUSE THREE MONTHS NOW, AND YOU CAME FROM - ?

LOWOOD SCHOOL.

AH, A CHARITABLE CONCERN. HOW LONG WERE YOU THERE?

EIGHT YEARS, SIR.

EIGHT YEARS! YOU MUST BE TENACIOUS OF LIFE.

I THOUGHT HALF THE TIME IN SUCH A PLACE WOULD HAVE DONE UP ANY CONSTITUTION!

NO WONDER YOU HAVE RATHER THE LOOK OF ANOTHER WORLD.

WHEN YOU CAME ON ME IN HAY LANE LAST NIGHT, I THOUGHT UNACCOUNTABLY OF FAIRY TALES, AND HAD HALF A MIND TO DEMAND WHETHER YOU HAD BEWITCHED MY HORSE.

WHO ARE YOUR PARENTS?

I HAVE NONE.

NOR EVER HAD, I SUPPOSE. DO YOU REMEMBER THEM?

NO.

I THOUGHT NOT. AND SO YOU WERE WAITING FOR YOUR PEOPLE WHEN YOU SAT ON THAT STILE?

FOR WHOM, SIR?

FOR THE MEN IN GREEN. IT WAS A PROPER MOONLIGHT EVENING FOR THEM. DID I BREAK THROUGH ONE OF YOUR RINGS, THAT YOU SPREAD THAT DAMNED ICE ON THE CAUSEWAY?

THE **MEN** IN **GREEN FORSOOK** ENGLAND A **HUNDRED YEARS** AGO, AND NOT EVEN IN **HAY LANE**, OR THE **FIELDS ABOUT** IT, COULD YOU FIND A **TRACE** OF THEM.

I DON'T THINK EITHER **SUMMER** OR **HARVEST**, OR **WINTER MOON**, WILL **EVER** SHINE ON THEIR **REVELS** MORE.

WELL, IF YOU DISOWN **PARENTS**, YOU MUST HAVE SOME SORT OF **KINSFOLK**: **UNCLES** AND **AUNTS**?

NO; NONE THAT I EVER **SAW**; AND NO **BROTHERS** OR **SISTERS**

WHO **RECOMMENDED** YOU TO COME HERE?

I **ADVERTISED**, AND MRS. FAIRFAX **ANSWERED**.

YES, AND I AM DAILY **THANKFUL** FOR THE CHOICE **PROVIDENCE** LED ME TO **MAKE**. **MISS EYRE** HAS BEEN AN **INVALUABLE COMPANION** TO ME, AND A **KIND** AND **CAREFUL TEACHER** TO **ADÈLE**.

DON'T **TROUBLE YOURSELF** TO GIVE HER A **CHARACTER**. I SHALL **JUDGE** FOR **MYSELF**.

SIR?

I HAVE TO **THANK HER** FOR THIS **SPRAIN**.

MISS **EYRE**, HAVE YOU EVER SEEN MUCH **SOCIETY**?

NONE BUT THE **PUPILS** AND **TEACHERS** OF **LOWOOD**, AND NOW THE **INMATES** OF **THORNFIELD**.

HAVE YOU **READ** MUCH?

ONLY SUCH **BOOKS** AS **CAME** MY **WAY**, AND THEY HAVE NOT BEEN **NUMEROUS**, OR VERY **LEARNED**.

YOU HAVE LIVED THE LIFE OF A **NUN**: NO **DOUBT** YOU ARE WELL **DRILLED** IN **RELIGIOUS** FORMS; **BROCKLEHURST**, WHO I UNDERSTAND **DIRECTS** LOWOOD, IS A **PARSON**; AND YOU **GIRLS** PROBABLY **WORSHIPPED** HIM, AS A **CONVENT** FULL OF **RELIGIEUSES** WOULD WORSHIP THEIR **DIRECTOR**.

47

OH, NO.

YOU'RE VERY COOL. - NO!

WHAT? A NOVICE NOT WORSHIP HER PRIEST! THAT SOUNDS BLASPHEMOUS.

I DISLIKED MR. BROCKLEHURST. HE IS A HARSH MAN; AT ONCE POMPOUS AND MEDDLING; AND FOR ECONOMY'S SAKE BOUGHT US BAD NEEDLES AND THREAD.

THAT WAS VERY FALSE ECONOMY.

HE STARVED US BEFORE THE COMMITTEE WAS APPOINTED; AND HE BORED US WITH LONG LECTURES ONCE A WEEK ABOUT SUDDEN DEATHS AND JUDGMENTS, WHICH MADE US AFRAID TO GO TO BED.

YOU STAYED THERE FOR EIGHT YEARS: YOU ARE NOW, THEN, EIGHTEEN?

YES, SIR.

IT IS A POINT DIFFICULT TO FIX WHERE THE FEATURES AND COUNTENANCE ARE SO MUCH AT VARIANCE.

CAN YOU PLAY?

A LITTLE.

SIT DOWN TO THE PIANO AND PLAY A TUNE.

ENOUGH!

YOU PLAY A LITTLE, I SEE; LIKE ANY OTHER ENGLISH SCHOOL-GIRL;

PERHAPS RATHER BETTER THAN SOME, BUT NOT WELL.

ADÈLE SHOWED ME SOME SKETCHES THIS MORNING, WHICH SHE SAID WERE YOURS.

I DON'T KNOW WHETHER THEY WERE ENTIRELY OF YOUR DOING; PROBABLY A MASTER AIDED YOU.

NO, INDEED!

AH! THAT PRICKS PRIDE.

WHERE DID YOU GET YOUR **COPIES**?

OUT OF MY **HEAD**.

HAS IT **OTHER** FURNITURE OF THE **SAME KIND** WITHIN?

I SHOULD **HOPE - BETTER**.

THESE **EYES**, YOU MUST HAVE SEEN IN A **DREAM**.

AND WHO TAUGHT YOU TO PAINT **WIND**? THERE IS A **HIGH GALE** IN THAT SKY, AND ON THIS **HILL-TOP**. WHERE DID YOU SEE **LATMOS**? FOR **THAT** IS LATMOS.

AND YOU FELT **SELF-SATISFIED** WITH THE RESULT OF YOUR **ARDENT LABOURS**?

FAR **FROM IT**. I WAS **TORMENTED** BY THE CONTRAST BETWEEN MY **IDEAS** AND MY **HANDIWORK**.

I HAD **IMAGINED** THINGS I WAS QUITE **POWERLESS** TO **REALISE**.

YOU HAD NOT ENOUGH OF THE ARTIST'S **SKILL** AND **SCIENCE** TO GIVE IT FULL **BEING**, YET THE DRAWINGS **ARE**, FOR A **SCHOOLGIRL**, PECULIAR.

AS TO THE **THOUGHTS**, THEY ARE **ELFISH**.

AT NINE O'CLOCK, I PUT ADÈLE TO **BED** AND JOINED **MRS. FAIRFAX** IN HER **ROOM**.

I FIND **MR. ROCHESTER** VERY **CHANGEFUL** AND **ABRUPT**.

TRUE: NO DOUBT HE MAY **APPEAR** SO TO A **STRANGER**.

BUT I AM SO **ACCUSTOMED** TO HIS MANNER, I NEVER **THINK** OF IT; AND THEN, IF HE HAS **PECULARITIES**, **ALLOWANCE** SHOULD BE MADE.

WHY?

FAMILY TROUBLES, FOR ONE THING. OUR MASTER **EDWARD** INHERITED **THORNFIELD** ONLY **NINE YEARS** AGO, AFTER HIS BROTHER **ROWLAND** DIED.

THEIR FATHER WAS **ANXIOUS** THAT MASTER **EDWARD** HAD **WEALTH TOO**; AND, SOON AFTER HE WAS **OF AGE**, SOME **STEPS** WERE TAKEN THAT PUT MASTER EDWARD IN A **PAINFUL POSITION**.

I DON'T THINK HE HAS EVER BEEN **RESIDENT** AT **THORNFIELD** FOR A **FORTNIGHT TOGETHER**.

49

CHAPTER XIV

MA BOÎTE! MA BOÎTE!

SEVERAL **DAYS** PASSED WITH **LITTLE CONTACT** WITH **MR. ROCHESTER.**

YES, THERE IS YOUR "**BOÎTE**" AT LAST. TAKE IT INTO A **CORNER**, YOU GENUINE DAUGHTER OF **PARIS**, AND AMUSE YOURSELF WITH DISEMBOWELLING IT AND **MIND**, DON'T **BOTHER** ME WITH ANY **DETAILS OF THE ANATOMICAL PROCESS** LET YOUR **OPERATION** BE CONDUCTED IN **SILENCE**. TIENS-TOI **TRANQUILLE**, ENFANT; COMPRENDS-TU?

COME **FORWARD**, MISS **EYRE**; BE SEATED HERE.

I AM NOT **FOND** OF THE **PRATTLE** OF **CHILDREN**, OLD **BACHELOR** AS I AM. IT WOULD BE **INTOLERABLE** TO ME TO PASS A **WHOLE EVENING** WITH A **BRAT**.

DON'T DRAW THAT CHAIR **FARTHER OFF**, MISS **EYRE**. SIT DOWN **EXACTLY** WHERE I **PLACED** IT - IF YOU **PLEASE**, THAT IS. **CONFOUND** THESE CIVILITIES! I CONTINUALLY **FORGET** THEM. NOR DO I **PARTICULARLY** AFFECT **SIMPLE-MINDED OLD LADIES**...

CHING! CHING!

HE **RANG** AND DESPATCHED AN **INVITATION** TO MRS. FAIRFAX.

GOOD **EVENING**, MADAM; I SEN— TO YOU FOR A **CHARITABLE PURPOSE**. I HAVE **FORBIDDE**— ADÈLE TO TALK TO ME ABOUT HER **PRESENTS**.

HAVE THE **GOODNESS** TO SERVE HER AS **AUDITRESS** AND **INTERLOCUTRICE**; IT WILL BE ONE OF THE MOST **BENEVOLEN**— **ACTS** YOU EVER **PERFORMED**.

NOW I HAVE PERFORMED THE PART OF A **GOOD HOST**; PUT MY **GUESTS** INTO THE WAY OF **AMUSING** EACH OTHER.

YOU **EXAMINE** ME, MISS EYRE. DO YOU THINK ME **HANDSOME**?

NO, SIR.

AH! BY MY **WORD**! THERE IS SOMETHING **SINGULAR**— ABOUT YOU. YOU HAVE THE AIR OF A **LITTLE NONNETTE**, QUAINT, **QUIET, GRAVE** AND **SIMPLE**; AND **WHEN** ONE MAKES A **REMARK** TO WHICH YOU ARE **OBLIGED** TO **REPLY**, YOU RAP OUT A **ROUND REJOINDER**, WHICH, IF NOT BLUNT, IS AT LEAST **BRUSQUE**.

SIR, I WAS TOO **PLAIN**; I BEG YOUR **PARDON**. I **OUGHT** TO HAVE REPLIED THAT **TASTES** MOSTLY **DIFFER**, AND THAT **BEAUTY** IS OF LITTLE **CONSEQUENCE**, OR SOMETHING OF THAT SORT.

YOU **OUGHT** TO HAVE REPLIED **NO SUCH THING.**

BEAUTY OF LITTLE **CONSEQUENCE**, INDEED!

AND **SO**, UNDER **PRETENCE** OF SOFTENING THE **PREVIOUS** OUTRAGE, YOU STICK A SLY **PENKNIFE** UNDER MY **EAR!**

CRITICISE ME: DOES MY **FOREHEAD** NOT **PLEASE** YOU? AM I A **FOOL?**

FAR **FROM** IT, SIR. YOU WOULD, PERHAPS, THINK ME **RUDE** IF I INQUIRED WHETHER YOU ARE A **PHILANTHROPIST?**

THERE **AGAIN!** ANOTHER STICK OF THE **PENKNIFE.** NO, YOUNG LADY, I AM **NOT** A GENERAL **PHILANTHROPIST**, BUT I BEAR A **CONSCIENCE.**

FORTUNE HAS KNOCKED ME **ABOUT**, AND **NOW** I **FLATTER** MYSELF I AM **HARD** AND **TOUGH** AS AN INDIA-RUBBER **BALL** - THOUGH WITH **ONE SENTIENT POINT** IN THE **MIDDLE** OF THE **LUMP.**

DOES THAT LEAVE **HOPE** FOR ME?

HOPE OF **WHAT**, SIR?

OF MY FINAL **RE-TRANSFORMATION** FROM **INDIA-RUBBER** BACK TO **FLESH?**

YOU LOOK VERY MUCH **PUZZLED**, MISS **EYRE**:

AND THOUGH YOU ARE NOT **PRETTY**, ANY MORE THAN I AM **HANDSOME**, YET A PUZZLED AIR **BECOMES** YOU;

BESIDES, IT IS **CONVENIENT**, FOR IT KEEPS THOSE **SEARCHING EYES** OF YOURS AWAY FROM MY **PHYSIOGNOMY**, AND BUSIES THEM WITH THE **WORSTED FLOWERS** OF THE **RUG**; SO PUZZLE ON.

YOUNG **LADY,** I AM **DISPOSED** TO BE **GREGARIOUS** AND **COMMUNICATIVE** TONIGHT, AND THAT IS WHY I **SENT** FOR YOU. IT WOULD **PLEASE** ME NOW TO **DRAW YOU OUT** - TO LEARN **MORE** OF YOU - THEREFORE, **SPEAK.**

INSTEAD OF **SPEAKING,** I **SMILED.**

SPEAK.

WHAT **ABOUT,** SIR?

WHATEVER YOU **LIKE.**

I LEAVE THE CHOICE OF **SUBJECT** ENTIRELY TO **YOURSELF.**

IF HE EXPECTS ME TO **TALK** FOR THE MERE SAKE OF **TALKING** AND **SHOWING OFF,** HE WILL FIND HE HAS **ADDRESSED** HIMSELF TO THE **WRONG PERSON.**

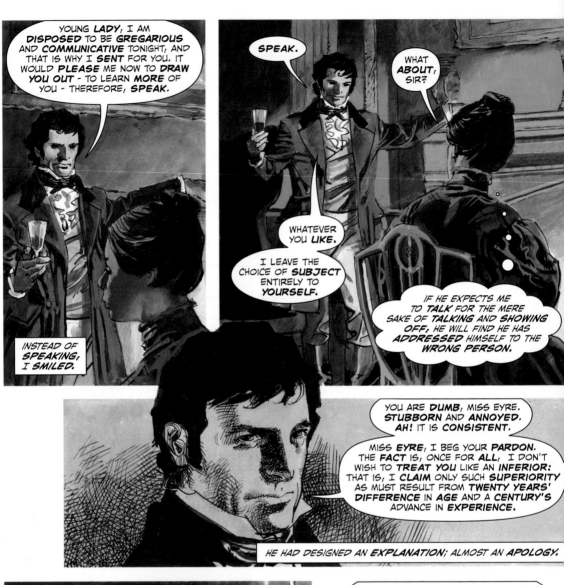

YOU ARE **DUMB,** MISS EYRE. **STUBBORN** AND **ANNOYED.** AH! IT IS **CONSISTENT.**

MISS **EYRE,** I BEG YOUR **PARDON.** THE **FACT** IS, ONCE FOR **ALL,** I DON'T WISH TO **TREAT YOU** LIKE AN **INFERIOR;** THAT IS, I **CLAIM** ONLY SUCH **SUPERIORITY** AS MUST RESULT FROM **TWENTY YEARS'** **DIFFERENCE** IN **AGE** AND A **CENTURY'S** ADVANCE IN **EXPERIENCE.**

HE HAD DESIGNED AN **EXPLANATION;** ALMOST AN **APOLOGY.**

DO YOU **AGREE** THAT I HAVE A **RIGHT** TO BE **MASTERFUL, ABRUPT,** PERHAPS **EXACTING,** SOMETIMES?

DO AS YOU **PLEASE,** SIR.

THAT IS **NO ANSWER;** OR RATHER IT IS A VERY **IRRITATING,** BECAUSE A VERY **EVASIVE,** ONE.

REPLY **CLEARLY.**

I DON'T **THINK,** SIR, YOU HAVE A RIGHT TO **COMMAND** ME, MERELY BECAUSE YOU ARE **OLDER** THAN I, OR BECAUSE YOU HAVE SEEN **MORE** OF THE WORLD THAN I HAVE; YOUR CLAIM TO **SUPERIORITY** DEPENDS ON THE **USE** YOU HAVE MADE OF YOUR **TIME** AND **EXPERIENCE.**

HUMPH! PROMPTLY SPOKEN.

BUT I WON'T ALLOW THAT AS I HAVE MADE AN INDIFFERENT USE OF BOTH ADVANTAGES.

LEAVING SUPERIORITY OUT OF THE QUESTION, THEN, YOU MUST STILL AGREE TO RECEIVE MY ORDERS NOW AND THEN, WITHOUT BEING PIQUED OR HURT BY THE TONE OF COMMAND. WILL YOU?

HE SEEMS TO FORGET THAT HE PAYS ME THIRTY POUNDS PER ANNUM FOR RECEIVING HIS ORDERS.

THE SMILE IS VERY WELL, BUT SPEAK, TOO.

I WAS THINKING THAT VERY FEW MASTERS WOULD TROUBLE THEMSELVES TO INQUIRE WHETHER OR NOT THEIR PAID SUBORDINATES WERE PIQUED AND HURT BY THEIR ORDERS.

PAID SUBORDINATES! WHAT! YOU ARE MY PAID SUBORDINATE, ARE YOU?

OH YES, I HAD FORGOTTEN THE SALARY! WELL, THEN, ON THAT MERCENARY GROUND, WILL YOU AGREE TO LET ME HECTOR A LITTLE?

NO, SIR, NOT ON THAT GROUND; BUT ON THE GROUND THAT YOU DID FORGET IT, AND THAT YOU CARE WHETHER OR NOT A DEPENDENT IS COMFORTABLE IN HIS DEPENDENCY, I AGREE HEARTILY.

AND WILL YOU CONSENT TO DISPENSE WITH A GREAT MANY CONVENTIONAL FORMS AND PHRASES, WITHOUT THINKING THAT THE OMISSION ARISES FROM INSOLENCE?

I AM **SURE**, SIR, I SHOULD NEVER MISTAKE **INFORMALITY** FOR **INSOLENCE**: ONE I RATHER **LIKE**, THE **OTHER** NOTHING **FREE-BORN** WOULD **SUBMIT** TO, EVEN **FOR A** SALARY.

HUMBUG! **MOST** THINGS **FREE-BORN** WILL SUBMIT TO **ANYTHING** FOR A **SALARY**.

HOWEVER, I MENTALLY **SHAKE HANDS** WITH YOU FOR YOUR ANSWER, **DESPITE** IT'S INACCURACY.

NOT **THREE** IN **THREE THOUSAND** RAW **SCHOOLGIRL-GOVERNESSES** WOULD HAVE ANSWERED ME AS **YOU** HAVE JUST DONE.

BUT I DON'T MEAN TO **FLATTER** YOU: IT IS NO MERIT OF **YOURS**. **NATURE** DID IT.

FOR WHAT I **YET** KNOW, YOU MAY HAVE **INTOLERABLE DEFECTS** TO COUNTERBALANCE YOUR FEW **GOOD POINTS**.

AND SO MAY **YOU**.

I HAVE **PLENTY** OF FAULTS OF MY **OWN**. I **MIGHT** HAVE BEEN AS GOOD AS **YOU**. NATURE **MEANT** ME TO BE, ON THE **WHOLE**, A **GOOD MAN**, MISS **EYRE**; AND YOU **SEE** I AM **NOT** SO.

WHEN FATE **WRONGED** ME, I HAD NOT THE **WISDOM** TO STAY **COOL**. DREAD **REMORSE**, MISS **EYRE**; REMORSE IS THE **POISON** OF **LIFE**.

REPENTANCE IS SAID TO BE ITS **CURE**, SIR.

ting ting ting

IT IS **NOT** ITS **CURE**. **REFORMATION** MAY BE ITS CURE.

I SEE YOU LAUGH **RARELY** AND YOU **FEAR** TO **SMILE**: BUT, IN **TIME**, I THINK YOU WILL LEARN TO BE **NATURAL** WITH ME, AS I FIND IT **IMPOSSIBLE** TO BE **CONVENTIONAL** WITH **YOU**.

ting ting ting ting ting

IT HAS STRUCK **NINE**, SIR. IT IS **ADÈLE'S** BEDTIME.

NEVER **MIND** - WAIT A **MINUTE**: ADÈLE IS NOT **READY** TO GO TO BED **YET**.

SHE PULLED OUT OF HER **BOX**, ABOUT **TEN MINUTES** AGO, A LITTLE PINK **FROCK**; **RAPTURE** LIT HER **FACE** AS SHE **UNFOLDED** IT. SHE IS NOW WITH **SOPHIE**, UNDERGOING A **ROBING PROCESS**.

IN A FEW **MINUTES** SHE WILL **RE-ENTER**, AND I **KNOW** WHAT I SHALL **SEE** - A **MINIATURE** OF **CÉLINE VARENS**, AS SHE USED TO APPEAR ON THE **BOARDS** AT THE **RISING OF** --

-- BUT NEVER MIND **THAT**

STAY NOW, TO SEE WHETHER IT WILL BE **REALISED**.

MONSIEUR, JE VOUS REMERCIE MILLE FOIS DE VOTRE **BONTÉ**. C'EST COMME CELA QUE **MAMA FAISAIT**, N'EST-CE PAS, MONSIEUR?

PRE-CISE-LY! AND, 'COMME CELA', SHE CHARMED MY **ENGLISH GOLD** OUT OF MY **BRITISH BREECHES**' POCKET.

I HAVE BEEN **GREEN**, TOO, **MISS EYRE** - AY, **GRASS GREEN**. MY **SPRING** IS **GONE**, BUT IT HAS **LEFT** ME THAT **FRENCH FLOWERET** ON MY **HANDS**, WHICH IN SOME MOODS, I WOULD BE **FAIN** BE **RID OF**. I **KEEP** IT AND **REAR** IT RATHER ON THE ROMAN CATHOLIC PRINCIPLE OF EXPIATING NUMEROUS **SINS** BY **ONE GOOD WORK**.

I'LL **EXPLAIN** ALL THIS SOME DAY.

MR. ROCHESTER *DID*, ON A *FUTURE* OCCASION, *EXPLAIN* IT.

ADÈLE WAS THE DAUGHTER OF A FRENCH OPERA-DANCER, *CÉLINE VARENS*, FOR WHOM I ONCE CHERISHED A *'GRANDE PASSION'*.

THIS *PASSION* CÉLINE PROFESSED TO *RETURN* WITH EVEN *SUPERIOR ARDOUR*.

~ CHAPTER XV ~

AND, MISS *EYRE*, SO *MUCH* WAS I FLATTERED BY THIS *PREFERENCE* OF THE *GALLIC SYLPH* FOR HER *BRITISH GNOME*, THAT I *INSTALLED* HER IN AN *HOTEL*; GAVE HER A COMPLETE *ESTABLISHMENT* OF *SERVANTS*, A *CARRIAGE*, *DIAMONDS* --

-- IN *SHORT*, I BEGAN THE *PROCESS* OF *RUINING MYSELF*.

HAPPENING TO *CALL* ONE EVENING WHEN *CÉLINE* DID NOT *EXPECT* ME, I FOUND HER *OUT*.

THE *BALCONY* WAS FURNISHED WITH A *CHAIR* OR TWO, AND I *SAT* THERE IN THE *WARM EVENING*.

THE *VOITURE* I HAD GIVEN HER ARRIVED AND MY *FLAME ALIGHTED* - I WAS ABOUT TO *CALL* HER WHEN A *FIGURE* JUMPED FROM THE CARRIAGE *AFTER* HER.

YOU NEVER FELT *JEALOUSY*, *DID* YOU, MISS *EYRE*?

OF *COURSE* NOT. BECAUSE YOU NEVER FELT *LOVE*.

BUT I *TELL* YOU, YOU WILL *COME* SOME DAY TO A *CRAGGY PASS*: EITHER YOU WILL BE *DASHED* TO *ATOMS*, OR LIFTED *UP* INTO A *CALMER* CURRENT - AS *I AM* NOW.

I *LIKE* THIS DAY. I LIKE THAT *SKY OF STEEL*.

I LIKE *THORNFIELD*; ITS GREY *FAÇADE*; AND YET HOW *LONG* HAVE I *SHUNNED* IT LIKE A GREAT *PLAGUE-HOUSE*?

HOW I DO STILL *ABHOR*...

HE GROUND HIS *TEETH* AND WAS SILENT. SOME *HATED THOUGHT* SEEMED TO HAVE HIM IN ITS *GRIP*.

DURING THE MOMENT I WAS **SILENT**, MISS **EYRE**, I WAS ARRANGING A **POINT** WITH MY **DESTINY**. SHE **STOOD** THERE, A **HAG** LIKE ONE OF THOSE WHO APPEARED TO **MACBETH**.

"YOU LIKE **THORNFIELD?**" SHE SAID AND **WROTE** IN THE **AIR** ALL ALONG THE HOUSE-FRONT:

"**LIKE** IT IF YOU **CAN!** LIKE IT IF YOU **DARE!**"

"I **WILL** LIKE IT", SAID I. "I **DARE** LIKE IT".

I WILL **BREAK** OBSTACLES TO **HAPPINESS**, TO **GOODNESS** - YES, **GOODNESS**.

DID YOU **LEAVE** THE **BALCONY**, SIR, WHEN MADEMOISELLE VARENS ENTERED?

OH, I HAD FORGOTTEN CÉLINE! **WELL**, TO **RESUME**, I REMAINED IN THE **BALCONY** AND DREW THE **CURTAIN**.

THE PAIR CAME **IN**, AND REMOVED THEIR **CLOAKS**. THERE WAS "*THE VARENS*" SHINING IN **SATIN** AND **JEWELS** - **MY** GIFTS OF COURSE - AND THERE WAS HER **COMPANION** IN AN **OFFICER'S** UNIFORM. I KNEW HIM - A **BRAINLESS**, VICIOUS YOUTH WHOM I **DESPISED**. OPENING THE **WINDOW**, I **WALKED** IN UPON THEM; **LIBERATED** CÉLINE FROM MY **PROTECTION**, DISREGARDED **SCREAMS** AND **HYSTERICS** AND MADE AN **APPOINTMENT** WITH THE **VICOMTE** FOR A **MEETING** AT THE **BOIS DE BOULOGNE**.

NEXT **MORNING** I HAD THE PLEASURE OF LEAVING A **BULLET** IN ONE OF HIS POOR ETIOLATED **ARMS**, **FEEBLE** AS THE WING OF A **CHICKEN**.

I **THOUGHT** I HAD **DONE** WITH THE **WHOLE CREW**. BUT **UNLUCKILY** THE *VARENS*, SIX MONTHS BEFORE, HAD GIVEN ME THIS **FILETTE**, **ADÈLE**, WHO, SHE AFFIRMED, WAS MY **DAUGHTER**.

PERHAPS SHE MAY BE, THOUGH I SEE NO **PROOFS** OF SUCH **GRIM PATERNITY** WRITTEN IN HER **COUNTENANCE**. HER MOTHER **ABANDONED** HER CHILD AND **RAN AWAY** TO **ITALY**.

I ACKNOWLEDGED NO **NATURAL CLAIM**, FOR I AM **NOT** HER **FATHER**; BUT HEARING THAT SHE WAS **DESTITUTE**, I **TRANSPLANTED** HER HERE.

NOW YOU **KNOW**, YOU WILL PERHAPS **BEG** ME TO LOOK OUT FOR A **NEW** GOVERNESS, EH?

NO: ADÈLE IS NOT **ANSWERABLE** FOR EITHER HER **MOTHER'S** FAULTS OR **YOURS**.

FORSAKEN BY HER **MOTHER** AND **DISOWNED** BY YOU, SIR - I SHALL **CLING CLOSER** TO HER THAN **BEFORE**.

I COULD NOT **SLEEP** FOR THINKING OF HIS **LOOK** WHEN HE TOLD HOW HIS **DESTINY** HAD **RISEN UP** BEFORE HIM.

I HARDLY KNOW WHETHER I HAD **SLEPT** OR **NOT** AFTER THIS MUSING WHEN I HEARD A **SOUND**...

EEE-EEE-AH-HA...

WHO IS THERE?

WAS THAT **GRACE POOLE?** AND IS SHE **POSSESSED** WITH A **DEVIL?**

THUD
THUD
THUD
THUD
CREAK
CLUNK

I THOUGHT AT **FIRST** THE GOBLIN LAUGHTER STOOD AT MY **BEDSIDE.** ERE **LONG,** STEPS RETREATED TOWARDS THE THIRD-STORY **STAIRCASE:** A DOOR **OPENED** AND **CLOSED,** AND ALL WAS **STILL.**

!

WAKE! WAKE!

HISSSSSS

IS THERE A **FLOOD**?

NO, SIR. BUT THERE **HAS** BEEN A **FIRE**.

IN THE NAME OF **ALL** THE **ELVES** IN **CHRISTENDOM**, IS THAT **JANE EYRE?** HAVE YOU PLOTTED TO **DROWN** ME?

SOMEBODY HAS PLOTTED **SOMETHING**. YOU CANNOT **TOO SOON** FIND OUT **WHO** AND **WHAT** IT WAS.

I BRIEFLY **RELATED** TO HIM WHAT HAD **TRANSPIRED**. HE LISTENED VERY **GRAVELY**; HIS **FACE** EXPRESSED MORE **CONCERN** THAN **ASTONISHMENT**.

REMAIN WHERE YOU **ARE** TILL I **RETURN**; BE AS **STILL** AS A **MOUSE**.

DON'T **MOVE**, REMEMBER, OR **CALL** ANYONE.

A VERY LONG TIME ELAPSED...

I HAVE **FOUND** IT ALL OUT. I **FORGET** WHETHER YOU SAID YOU **SAW** ANYTHING WHEN YOU **OPENED** YOUR **CHAMBER** DOOR.

ONLY THE **CANDLESTICK**.

BUT YOU **HEARD** AN **ODD LAUGH**?

YES, SIR: A **WOMAN** WHO **SEWS** HERE, CALLED **GRACE POOLE** - SHE LAUGHS THAT WAY.

JUST **SO**. **GRACE POOLE** - YOU HAVE **GUESSED** IT. SAY NOTHING ABOUT TO-NIGHT'S **INCIDENT**.

YOU HAVE **SAVED** MY **LIFE**. I HAVE A **PLEASURE** IN **OWING** YOU SO **IMMENSE** A **DEBT**.

GOOD-NIGHT, SIR.

THERE IS NO **DEBT**, **BENEFIT**, **OBLIGATION** IN THE **CASE**.

I **KNEW** YOU WOULD DO ME **GOOD** IN SOME WAY, AT **SOME** TIME.

MY **CHERISHED PRESERVER**, **GOOD-NIGHT**!

I AM **GLAD** I HAPPENED TO BE **AWAKE**.

I **THINK** I HEAR **MRS. FAIRFAX** MOVE, SIR.

WELL, LEAVE ME.

*I REGAINED MY **COUCH**, BUT NEVER THOUGHT OF **SLEEP**. TOO FEVERISH TO REST, I ROSE AS SOON AS **DAY DAWNED**.*

THE NEXT **MORNING**, I WAS **AMAZED** TO FIND **GRACE POOLE** SEWING **RINGS** TO NEW **CURTAINS** IN **MR. ROCHESTER'S** BEDROOM. THERE WAS **NO SIGN** OF **DESPERATION** FROM THE **WOMAN** WHO HAD ATTEMPTED **MURDER**.

~ CHAPTER XVI ~

MASTER HAD BEEN **READING** IN HIS **BED** LAST NIGHT;

HE FELL **ASLEEP** WITH HIS **CANDLE** LIT, AND THE **CURTAINS** GOT ON **FIRE**.

DID **MR. ROCHESTER** WAKE NOBODY?

THE **SERVANTS** SLEEP **TOO FAR AWAY**. **YOU'RE** NEAREST; PERHAPS **YOU** MAY HAVE HEARD A NOISE?

I AM **CERTAIN** I HEARD A **LAUGH**, AND A **STRANGE** ONE.

IT IS HARDLY **LIKELY** MASTER WOULD **LAUGH**, WHEN HE WAS IN SUCH **DANGER**: YOU MUST HAVE BEEN **DREAMING**.

I WAS **NOT DREAMING**.

I HAD **SO MANY THINGS** TO SAY TO **MR. ROCHESTER**! I WANTED **AGAIN** TO INTRODUCE THE SUBJECT OF **GRACE POOLE**, AND TO **HEAR** WHAT HE WOULD **ANSWER**; BUT I DIDN'T **HEAR** HIM IN THE **HOUSE**.

DIRECTLY AFTER **BREAKFAST**, **MR. ROCHESTER** SET OFF FOR **THE LEAS**, MR. **ESHTON'S** PLACE. THERE IS **QUITE** A **PARTY** THERE, AND IS **LIKELY** TO STAY A **WEEK** OR MORE.

ARE THERE **LADIES** AT **THE LEAS**?

THERE ARE **MRS. ESHTON** AND HER **THREE** DAUGHTERS; AND THERE ARE **BLANCHE** AND **MARY INGRAM**, I SUPPOSE.

BLANCHE WAS THE **BELLE** OF A **CHRISTMAS BALL** MR. **ROCHESTER** GAVE AROUND **SEVEN** YEARS AGO.

THEY **SANG** A **DUET**...

I WAS NOT **AWARE** THAT **MR. ROCHESTER** COULD **SING**.

HE HAS A **FINE BASS** VOICE.

AND MISS INGRAM?

A VERY RICH ONE.

I WONDER NO WEALTHY GENTLEMAN HAS TAKEN A FANCY TO HER: MR. ROCHESTER, FOR INSTANCE.

HE IS NEARLY FORTY; SHE IS BUT TWENTY-FIVE.

WHEN ONCE MORE ALONE, I REVIEWED THE INFORMATION I HAD GOT. A GREATER FOOL THAN JANE EYRE HAD NEVER BREATHED THE BREATH OF LIFE.

YOU, A FAVOURITE OF MR. ROCHESTER? GO! YOUR FOLLY SICKENS ME. POOR STUPID DOPE!

I SENTENCED MYSELF TO DRAW MY OWN PICTURE, WITHOUT SOFTENING ONE DEFECT...

PORTRAIT of a GOVERNESS, DISCONNECTED — POOR, AND PLAIN.

...AND THEN, WITH MY FINEST, CLEAREST TINTS, TO PAINT THE LOVELIEST FACE I COULD IMAGINE, AND CALL IT 'BLANCHE, AN ACCOMPLISHED LADY OF RANK'.

I DERIVED BENEFIT FROM THE TASK: IT HAD KEPT MY HEAD AND HANDS EMPLOYED. ERE LONG, I HAD REASON TO CONGRATULATE MYSELF ON THE COURSE OF WHOLESOME DISCIPLINE TO WHICH I HAD THUS FORCED MY FEELINGS TO SUBMIT.

~ CHAPTER XVII ~

MR. ROCHESTER HAD BEEN **ABSENT** UPWARDS OF A **FORTNIGHT**, WHEN THE **POST** BROUGHT **MRS. FAIRFAX** A LETTER.

MR. ROCHESTER IS NOT LIKELY TO **RETURN** SOON, I **SUPPOSE**?

INDEED HE **IS** - IN **THREE DAYS**; AND NOT **ALONE** EITHER.

HE SENDS **DIRECTIONS** FOR ALL THE **BEST BEDROOMS** TO BE PREPARED; AND **ROOMS** TO BE **CLEANED OUT**.

THE THREE DAYS WERE **BUSY ENOUGH**. THREE **WOMEN** WERE GOT TO **HELP**. **ADÈLE** RAN **QUITE WILD** IN THE **MIDST** OF IT: THE **PREPARATIONS** AND THE PROSPECT OF **COMPANY** SEEMED TO THROW HER INTO **ECSTASIES**.

MRS. FAIRFAX HAD **PRESSED** ME INTO HER **SERVICE**, AND I WAS **ALL DAY** HELPING (OR **HINDERING**) HER AND THE **COOK**.

GRACE POOLE SPENT **MOST** OF THE TIME IN SOME **CHAMBER** OF THE **THIRD STORY**: THERE SHE **SAT** AND SEWED...

...AS **COMPANIONLESS** AS A **PRISONER** IN HIS **DUNGEON**.

THE **DAY CAME**: ALL **WORK** HAD BEEN **COMPLETED** THE **PREVIOUS EVENING**.

IT GETS **LATE**.

I AM **GLAD** I ORDERED **DINNER** AN **HOUR** AFTER THE TIME MR. ROCHESTER MENTIONED.

MISS INGRAM!

THE FOLLOWING **EVENING**, MR. ROCHESTER INSISTED THAT I **ACCOMPANY** ADÈLE TO THE DRAWING-ROOM AFTER **DINNER**.

A **BAND** OF LADIES ENTERED AND THE **CURTAIN** FELL **BEHIND** THEM.

BON JOUR, MESDAMES.

OH, WHAT A LITTLE **PUPPET**!

IT IS **MR. ROCHESTER'S WARD**, I SUPPOSE - THE **LITTLE FRENCH GIRL** HE WAS **SPEAKING** OF.

WHAT A **LOVE** OF A **CHILD**!

AT LAST **COFFEE** IS BROUGHT IN, AND THE **GENTLEMEN** ARE SUMMONED. I SIT IN THE **SHADE**; THE **WINDOW-CURTAIN** HALF **HIDES** ME.

AND **WHERE** IS MR. **ROCHESTER**?

HE COMES IN **LAST**: I AM NOT **LOOKING**, YET I **SEE** HIM ENTER.

CONVERSATION WAXES **BRISK** AND **MERRY**. **HENRY**, THE SON OF **LADY LYNN** IS TRYING TO TALK **FRENCH** WITH **ADÈLE**, AND **LOUISA ESHTON** LAUGHS AT HIS **BLUNDERS**.

THE TWO PROUD **DOWAGERS**, LADY **LYNN** AND LADY **INGRAM**, **CONFABULATE** TOGETHER;

SIR **GEORGE** OCCASIONALLY PUTS IN A **WORD**.

COLONEL **DENT** AND MR. **ESHTON** ARGUE ABOUT **POLITICS**; THEIR **WIVES** LISTEN.

LORD **INGRAM** LEANS ON THE **CHAIR-BACK** OF AMY **ESHTON**;

SHE LIKES **HIM** BETTER THAN SHE DOES **MR. ROCHESTER**.

I COMPARED MR. **ROCHESTER** WITH HIS **GUESTS**. I SAW THEM **SMILE**, **LAUGH** - IT WAS **NOTHING**; I SAW MR. **ROCHESTER** SMILE - HIS **STERN** FEATURES **SOFTENED**.

HE IS NOT TO **THEM** WHAT HE IS TO **ME**.

I MUST **REMEMBER** THAT HE CANNOT **CARE** MUCH FOR ME - AND YET, WHILE I **BREATHE** AND **THINK**, I MUST **LOVE** HIM.

WHENEVER I MARRY, I AM **RESOLVED** MY **HUSBAND** SHALL NOT BE A **RIVAL**, BUT A **FOIL** TO ME. I SHALL **SUFFER** NO **COMPETITOR** NEAR THE **THRONE.**

MR. **ROCHESTER**, NOW **SING**, AND I WILL **PLAY** FOR YOU.

I AM ALL **OBEDIENCE.**

NOW IS MY **TIME** TO **SLIP AWAY.**

BUT THE **TONES** THAT THEN **SEVERED** THE **AIR ARRESTED** ME.

I **WAITED** TILL THE **LAST** DEEP AND **FULL VIBRATION** OF MR. **ROCHESTER'S** FINE **VOICE** HAD **EXPIRED** AND MADE MY **EXIT.**

OUTSIDE, I **STOPPED** TO TIE MY SANDAL...

WHY DID YOU NOT COME AND **SPEAK** TO ME IN THE **ROOM?**

YOU **SEEMED ENGAGED,** SIR.

YOU ARE **DESERTING** TOO **EARLY.**

I AM **TIRED,** SIR.

AND A LITTLE **DEPRESSED.** WHAT ABOUT?

NOTHING, SIR.

I AM NOT **DEPRESSED.**

BUT I **AFFIRM** THAT YOU **ARE** - SO MUCH DEPRESSED THAT A **FEW MORE WORDS** WOULD BRING **TEARS** TO YOUR **EYES.**

WELL, **TO-NIGHT** I **EXCUSE** YOU; BUT WHILE MY **VISITORS** STAY, I **EXPECT** YOU TO APPEAR IN THE **DRAWING-ROOM** EVERY **EVENING.**

IT IS MY **WISH.**

GOODNIGHT, MY --

HE **STOPPED,** BIT HIS **LIP,** AND **ABRUPTLY LEFT** ME.

MERRY DAYS WERE **THESE** AT **THORNFIELD HALL**. ALL **SAD FEELINGS** SEEMED NOW **DRIVEN** FROM THE **HOUSE**. EVEN WHEN **RAIN** SET IN, INDOOR **AMUSEMENTS** BECAME MORE **LIVELY,** LIKE **'CHARADES'**.

~ CHAPTER XVIII ~

BRIDEWELL!

I HAD **LEARNT** TO **LOVE** MR. **ROCHESTER**. I COULD NOT **UN-LOVE** HIM NOW, **MERELY** BECAUSE HE HAD CEASED TO **NOTICE** ME. I SAW **ALL HIS** ATTENTIONS APPROPRIATED BY MISS INGRAM.

VOILÀ, MONSIEUR ROCHESTER!

IT IS **NOT** MR. ROCHESTER, YOU **TIRESOME MONKEY!**

I WAS NOT **JEALOUS**: SHE WAS TOO **INFERIOR** TO **EXCITE** THE **FEELING**. SHE WAS VERY **SHOWY,** BUT SHE WAS NOT **GENUINE**. SHE COULD NOT **CHARM** HIM.

SOON, THE **NEW-COMER** ENTERED. HIS **MANNER** WAS **POLITE**, AND HE WAS A **FINE-LOOKING** MAN, AT **FIRST SIGHT** ESPECIALLY.

IT **APPEARS** I COME AT AN **INOPPORTUNE TIME**, MADAM, WHEN MY **FRIEND,** MR. ROCHESTER, IS **FROM HOME;**

BUT I **ARRIVE** FROM THE **WEST INDIES**, AND I THINK I MAY **PRESUME** TO **INSTALL MYSELF** HERE TILL HE **RETURNS.**

I **PRESENTLY** GATHERED THAT THE **NEW-COMER** WAS CALLED **MR. MASON.**

AFTER DINNER...

LADIES, **SAM**, HERE SAYS THAT A **GIPSY** IS IN THE **SERVANTS'** HALL, AND INSISTS UPON TELLING OUR **FORTUNES**.

DISMISS HER, BY **ALL MEANS,** AT **ONCE!**

BUT WE **CANNOT** PERSUADE HER TO GO AWAY, MY LADY.

SHE **SWEARS** SHE MUST **TELL THE GENTRY** THEIR **FORTUNES.**

SHE'LL HAVE **NO GENTLEMEN,** NOR **ANY LADIES,** EXCEPT THE **YOUNG** AND **SINGLE.**

TELL HER SHE SHALL BE **PUT** IN THE **STOCKS** IF SHE **DOESN'T LEAVE.**

I CANNOT **POSSIBLY** COUNTENANCE THIS.

INDEED, MAMA, BUT YOU **CAN** AND **WILL.**

I HAVE A **CURIOSITY** TO **HEAR** MY **FORTUNE** TOLD. I GO FIRST.

FIFTEEN MINUTES **LATER**...

WELL, BLANCHE?

I HAVE **SEEN A GIPSY VAGABOND.**

SHE HAS **TOLD ME** WHAT **SUCH** PEOPLE **USUALLY** TELL.

MY **WHIM** IS **GRATIFIED;** AND **NOW** I THINK **MR. ESHTON** WILL DO **WELL** TO PUT THE **HAG** IN THE **STOCKS TO-MORROW** MORNING, AS HE **THREATENED.**

NEXT, **MARY INGRAM, AMY** AND **LOUISA ESHTON** WENT **TOGETHER** AND **RETURNED** HALF-**SCARED** OUT OF THEIR **WITS.**

IF YOU **PLEASE,** MISS, THE **GIPSY** DECLARES THAT THERE IS **ANOTHER** YOUNG SINGLE LADY IN THE ROOM WHO HAS **NOT BEEN** TO HER YET.

I **THOUGHT** IT MUST BE **YOU.** WHAT SHALL I TELL HER?

OH, I WILL **GO** BY **ALL MEANS.** I AM **NOT** IN THE **LEAST AFRAID.**

THERE WAS *NOTHING INDEED* IN THE *GIPSY'S* APPEARANCE TO *TROUBLE* ONE'S *CALM*. WE WERE *SOON* DISCUSSING MR. *ROCHESTER*...

IS IT *KNOWN* THAT MR. *ROCHESTER* IS TO BE *MARRIED?*

YES; AND TO THE *BEAUTIFUL* MISS INGRAM.

HE *MUST* LOVE SUCH A *HANDSOME, NOBLE, WITTY, ACCOMPLISHED LADY;* AND *PROBABLY* SHE LOVES *HIM,* OR, IF NOT HIS *PERSON,* AT LEAST HIS *PURSE.*

THOUGH - GOD *PARDON* ME! - I *TOLD* HER SOMETHING ON *THAT* POINT WHICH MADE HER LOOK *WONDROUS GRAVE.*

~ CHAPTER XIX ~

SUDDENLY I SAW A BROAD RING WITH A GEM I HAD SEEN A HUNDRED TIMES BEFORE. THE BONNET WAS DOFFED, AND THE HEAD ADVANCED.

DO YOU *FORGIVE* ME, JANE?

I SHALL *TRY* TO FORGIVE YOU; BUT IT WAS *NOT RIGHT.*

I HAVE *PERMISSION* TO RETIRE NOW, I SUPPOSE?

NO; STAY A MOMENT; AND *TELL* ME WHAT THE PEOPLE IN THE *DRAWING-ROOM* ARE DOING.

DISCUSSING THE *GIPSY,* I *DARESAY.*

OH, ARE YOU *AWARE* THAT A *STRANGER* ARRIVED HERE?

DID HE GIVE HIS *NAME?*

MASON.

MASON!

-- FROM THE *WEST INDIES!*

DO YOU FEEL *ILL,* SIR? OH, *LEAN ON* ME, SIR.

MY LITTLE *FRIEND,* I WISH I WERE IN A *QUIET ISLAND* WITH ONLY YOU;

AND *TROUBLE,* AND *DANGER* AND *HIDEOUS* RECOLLECTIONS *REMOVED* FROM ME.

~ CHAPTER XX ~

THAT NIGHT...

ARRRGAH!!! EEiiGHH!!

GOOD GOD! WHAT A CRY!

IT *CAME* OUT OF THE *THIRD STORY;* FOR IT PASSED *OVERHEAD.*

I NOW HEARD A *STRUGGLE:* A *DEADLY* ONE IT SEEMED FROM THE *NOISE.*

HELP! HELP! HELP!

ROCHESTER!

FOR *GOD'S SAKE,* COME!

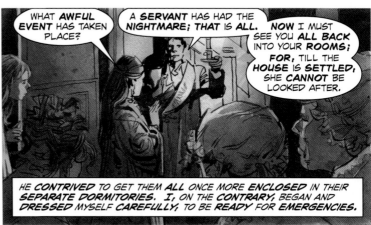

WHAT *AWFUL* EVENT HAS TAKEN PLACE?

A *SERVANT* HAS HAD THE *NIGHTMARE; THAT* IS *ALL.* NOW I MUST SEE YOU *ALL BACK* INTO YOUR *ROOMS; FOR,* TILL THE *HOUSE* IS *SETTLED,* SHE *CANNOT* BE LOOKED AFTER.

HE *CONTRIVED* TO GET THEM *ALL* ONCE MORE *ENCLOSED* IN THEIR *SEPARATE DORMITORIES.* I, ON THE *CONTRARY,* BEGAN AND *DRESSED* MYSELF *CAREFULLY;* TO BE *READY* FOR *EMERGENCIES.*

STILLNESS RETURNED; AND IN ABOUT AN *HOUR THORNFIELD HALL* WAS AGAIN AS *HUSHED* AS THE *DESERT.*

A *CAUTIOUS HAND* TAPPED *LOW* AT THE *DOOR.*

I want you. Come this way and make no noise.

Bring a sponge and any volatile salts you may have.

GRR-RR, RUGG-LL, HAAG!

YOU DON'T TURN *SICK* AT THE *SIGHT* OF *BLOOD?*

I THINK I SHALL NOT. I HAVE *NEVER* BEEN *TRIED* YET.

GIVE ME YOUR *HAND.* IT WILL NOT *DO* TO *RISK* A *FAINTING FIT.*

MR. MASON!

JANE, I SHALL HAVE TO **LEAVE YOU** IN **HERE** WHILE I FETCH A **SURGEON**.

SPONGE THE **BLOOD**; IF HE FEELS **FAINT**, YOU WILL PUT THE **GLASS OF WATER** TO HIS **LIPS** AND YOUR **SALTS** TO HIS **NOSE**.

IS THERE **IMMEDIATE DANGER**?

POOH! NO - A MERE **SCRATCH**. BEAR UP, MAN!

JANE, DO NOT **SPEAK** TO HIM ON **ANY PRETEXT**

- AND -

RICHARD, IT WILL BE AT THE **PERIL** OF YOUR **LIFE** IF **YOU** SPEAK TO HER. IF YOU **DO**, I'LL NOT **ANSWER** FOR THE **CONSEQUENCES**.

TWO HOURS **LATER**, MR. **ROCHESTER** RETURNED WITH THE **SURGEON**.

SHE'S **DONE** FOR ME, I **FEAR**! ROCHESTER GOT THE **KNIFE** FROM HER.

THERE HAVE BEEN **TEETH** HERE!

SHE **SUCKED** THE **BLOOD**: SHE SAID SHE'D **DRAIN** MY **HEART**.

NEVER MIND HER **GIBBERISH**: DON'T REPEAT IT.

HURRY!

I MUST HAVE HIM **OFF** BEFORE **SUNRISE**.

AT HALF-PAST **FIVE**, MR. **MASON** WAS **ASSISTED** INTO THE **CHAISE**.

LET HER BE **TAKEN CARE OF**: LET HER BE **TREATED** AS **TENDERLY** AS MAY BE; LET HER -

sob

sob

I DO MY **BEST**; AND **HAVE** DONE IT, AND **WILL** DO IT.

70

HA!

TELL HIM TO BE CAUTIOUS AND AVERT THE DANGER.

I MUST KEEP HIM IGNORANT THAT HARM TO ME IS POSSIBLE!

NOW YOU LOOK PUZZLED; AND I WILL PUZZLE YOU FURTHER.

YOU ARE MY LITTLE FRIEND, ARE YOU NOT?

I LIKE TO SERVE AND OBEY YOU, SIR.

WELL THEN, SUPPOSE YOU WERE A WILD BOY, INDULGED FROM CHILDHOOD, IN A REMOTE FOREIGN LAND; AND YOU COMMIT A CAPITAL ERROR - MIND I DON'T SAY A CRIME - WHOSE CONSEQUENCES MUST FOLLOW YOU THROUGH LIFE AND TAINT ALL YOUR EXISTENCE.

YOU COME HOME AFTER YEARS OF VOLUNTARY BANISHMENT, AND MEET A STRANGER WITH THE GOOD QUALITIES YOU SOUGHT FOR TWENTY YEARS.

IS THE SINFUL, BUT REPENTANT, WANDERER JUSTIFIED IN DARING THE WORLD'S OPINION, IN ORDER TO ATTACH TO HIM FOR EVER THIS GENTLE, GRACIOUS, GENIAL STRANGER, THEREBY SECURING HIS OWN PEACE OF MIND?

SIR, A SINNER'S REFORMATION SHOULD NEVER DEPEND ON A FELLOW-CREATURE.

IF ANY YOU KNOW HAS SUFFERED AND ERRED, LET HIM LOOK HIGHER THAN HIS EQUALS FOR STRENGTH TO AMEND AND SOLACE TO HEAL.

GOD, WHO DOES THE WORK, ORDAINS THE INSTRUMENT!

I HAVE MYSELF BEEN A WORLDLY, DISSIPATED, RESTLESS MAN, AND I BELIEVE I HAVE FOUND THE INSTRUMENT FOR MY CURE IN --

-- MISS INGRAM!

DON'T YOU THINK IF I MARRIED HER SHE WOULD REGENERATE ME WITH A VENGEANCE?

JANE, YOU ARE QUITE PALE. DON'T YOU CURSE ME FOR DISTURBING YOUR REST?

CURSE YOU? NO, SIR.

~ CHAPTER XXI ~

THAT *AFTERNOON* I RECEIVED A *VISITOR*.

MISSIS HAD BEEN *OUT* OF HEALTH HERSELF FOR *SOME TIME*.

THE *INFORMATION* ABOUT *MR. JOHN'S DEATH* BROUGHT ON A *STROKE*.

SHE WAS *THREE DAYS* WITHOUT *SPEAKING*; BUT *NOW* SHE KEEPS SAYING TO *BESSIE*, "*BRING JANE - FETCH JANE EYRE*".

IF YOU CAN *GET READY*, MISS, I SHOULD LIKE TO *TAKE* YOU *BACK* WITH ME.

I *DARESAY* YOU HARDLY *REMEMBER* ME, MISS. MY NAME IS *LEAVEN*: I LIVED *COACHMAN* WITH MRS. *REED* WHEN YOU WERE AT *GATESHEAD*.

OH, *ROBERT!* I *REMEMBER* YOU VERY *WELL*.

HOW IS YOUR *WIFE BESSIE*, AND THE *FAMILY* AT THE *HOUSE?*

MY *WIFE* IS VERY *HEARTY*, THANK YOU. I AM *SORRY* TO SAY, *MR. JOHN* DIED LAST WEEK. HE RUINED HIS *HEALTH* AND HIS *ESTATE* WITH THE *WORST MEN* AND *WOMEN*. HE WAS IN *DEBT*; HIS *MOTHER* WOULDN'T *HELP* HIM, *AND* THEY SAY HE *KILLED* HIMSELF.

I WENT IN *SEARCH* OF MR. *ROCHESTER*, TO *ASK* FOR LEAVE OF *ABSENCE*.

DOES *THAT PERSON WANT* YOU?

I *TOLD* HIM ABOUT *MRS. REED* AND WHAT HAD *HAPPENED*.

...BUT *GATESHEAD* IS A *HUNDRED MILES* OFF! MRS. *REED* SENDS FOR PEOPLE TO *SEE* HER THAT *DISTANCE*?

THERE WAS A *REED* OF *GATESHEAD*, A *MAGISTRATE*.

IT IS HIS *WIDOW*, SIR - AND MY *UNCLE*.

THE *DEUCE* HE *WAS!* *YOU* ALWAYS *SAID* YOU HAD *NO RELATIONS*.

NONE THAT WOULD *OWN* ME, SIR. SHE *CAST* ME OFF BECAUSE SHE *DISLIKED* ME; BUT *THAT* IS *LONG AGO*. I COULD NOT EASILY *NEGLECT* HER *WISHES* NOW.

I REACHED *GATESHEAD* ON THE *FIRST* OF *MAY*. THE *SAME* HOSTILE *ROOF* NOW *ROSE BEFORE* ME. I *STILL* FELT AS A *WANDERER* ON THE *FACE* OF THE *EARTH*; BUT I EXPERIENCED *FIRMER TRUST* IN *MYSELF* AND MY *OWN POWERS*. THE INANIMATE *OBJECTS* WERE NOT *CHANGED*; BUT THE *LIVING THINGS* HAD *ALTERED* PAST *RECOGNITION*.

HOW IS MRS. *REED?*

AH! MAMA, YOU MEAN; SHE IS *EXTREMELY POORLY*; I *DOUBT* IF YOU CAN *SEE* HER TONIGHT.

I MET *BESSIE* ON THE *LANDING* ON THE WAY TO MY *CHAMBER*, AND SHE *TOOK* ME TO SEE *MRS. REED*.

A MONTH ELAPSED BEFORE I QUITTED GATESHEAD.

GEORGIANA MADE AN ADVANTAGEOUS MATCH WITH A WEALTHY, WORN-OUT MAN OF FASHION.

ELIZA TOOK THE VEIL AND IS AT THIS DAY SUPERIOR OF THE CONVENT WHERE SHE PASSED THE PERIOD OF HER NOVITIATE, AND WHICH SHE ENDOWED WITH HER FORTUNE.

~ CHAPTER XXII ~

MY RETURN JOURNEY TO THORNFIELD SEEMED TEDIOUS. I FELT GLAD AS THE ROAD SHORTENED BEFORE ME. IT WAS PLEASURE ENOUGH TO HAVE THE PRIVILEGE OF AGAIN LOOKING AT MR. ROCHESTER, WHETHER HE LOOKED ON ME OR NOT.

HASTEN! BE WITH HIM WHILE YOU MAY: BUT A FEW MORE DAYS OR WEEKS, AT MOST, AND YOU ARE PARTED FROM HIM FOR EVER!

HOLLO!

THERE YOU ARE!

AND THIS IS JANE EYRE? COMING FROM MILLCOTE, AND ON FOOT?

YES - JUST ONE OF YOUR TRICKS: TO STEAL INTO THE VICINAGE OF YOUR HOME ALONG WITH TWILIGHT, JUST AS IF YOU WERE A DREAM.

WHAT THE DEUCE HAVE YOU DONE WITH YOURSELF THIS LAST MONTH?

I HAVE BEEN WITH MY AUNT, SIR, WHO IS DEAD.

A TRUE JANIAN REPLY! SHE COMES FROM THE OTHER WORLD - FROM THE ABODE OF PEOPLE WHO ARE DEAD; AND TELLS ME SO WHEN SHE MEETS ME ALONE HERE IN THE GLOAMING!

IF I DARED, I'D TOUCH YOU, TO SEE IF YOU ARE SUBSTANCE OR SHADOW, YOU ELF!

TRUANT! ABSENT FROM ME A WHOLE MONTH, AND FORGETTING ME QUITE, I'LL BE SWORN.

I KNEW THERE WOULD BE PLEASURE IN MEETING MY MASTER AGAIN.

HAVE YOU NOT BEEN TO **LONDON** TO BUY A NEW **CARRIAGE?**

YES; I SUPPOSE YOU FOUND **THAT** OUT BY **SECOND-SIGHT.** YOU MUST **SEE** THE **CARRIAGE, JANE,** AND **TELL** ME IF YOU **DON'T** THINK IT WILL **SUIT** MRS. **ROCHESTER EXACTLY.**

I WISH I WERE A TRIFLE BETTER **ADAPTED** TO **MATCH** WITH HER **EXTERNALLY.**

FAIRY AS YOU **ARE,** CAN'T YOU GIVE ME A **CHARM** TO MAKE ME A **HANDSOME MAN?**

IT WOULD BE **PAST** THE **POWER** OF **MAGIC,** SIR.

A LOVING EYE IS ALL THE **CHARM** NEEDED.

STAY YOUR **WEARY** LITTLE **WANDERING** FEET AT A **FRIEND'S THRESHOLD.**

THANK YOU, MR. **ROCHESTER,** FOR YOUR **GREAT KINDNESS.** I AM **STRANGELY GLAD** TO GET **BACK** AGAIN TO YOU.

WHEREVER YOU **ARE** IS MY **HOME -** MY ONLY **HOME.**

ADÈLE WAS **HALF WILD** WITH **DELIGHT** WHEN SHE **SAW** ME. MRS. FAIRFAX RECEIVED ME WITH HER **USUAL FRIENDLINESS.**

THERE IS NO **HAPPINESS** LIKE THAT OF BEING **LOVED** BY YOUR **FELLOW-CREATURES;** AND, **ALAS! NEVER** HAD I LOVED **HIM** SO **WELL.**

~ CHAPTER XXIII ~

ON **MIDSUMMER-EVE, ADÈLE, WEARY** WITH GATHERING **WILD STRAWBERRIES,** HAD GONE TO **BED** WITH THE **SUN.** I WATCHED HER DROP **ASLEEP,** AND WHEN I **LEFT** HER, I SOUGHT THE **GARDEN.**

THIS **SCENT** IS NEITHER **SHRUB** NOR **FLOWER.**

I KNOW IT **WELL -** IT IS MR. **ROCHESTER'S** CIGAR.

I MADE NO *NOISE*: HE HAD NOT *EYES* BEHIND - COULD HIS *SHADOW* FEEL?

JANE, COME AND LOOK AT *THIS FELLOW*. LOOK AT HIS *WINGS*. HE *REMINDS* ME RATHER OF A *WEST INDIAN* INSECT.

JANE, *THORNFIELD* IS A *PLEASANT* PLACE IN *SUMMER*; IS IT *NOT*?

YES, SIR.

YOU *MUST* HAVE BECOME IN *SOME* DEGREE *ATTACHED* TO THE HOUSE.

I AM *ATTACHED* TO IT, INDEED.

PITY. IT IS ALWAYS THE *WAY* OF EVENTS IN THIS *LIFE*.

NO *SOONER* HAVE YOU GOT *SETTLED*, THAN A *VOICE* CALLS *OUT* TO YOU TO *MOVE ON*.

MUST I *MOVE ON*, SIR? MUST I *LEAVE THORNFIELD*?

I BELIEVE YOU *MUST*, JANE.

IN A *MONTH* I *HOPE* TO BE A *BRIDEGROOM*. *ADÈLE* MUST GO TO *SCHOOL*; AND *YOU*, MISS *EYRE*, MUST GET A *NEW SITUATION*. I HAVE *ALREADY*, THROUGH MY *FUTURE MOTHER-IN-LAW*, HEARD OF A *PLACE* THAT I THINK WILL *SUIT*:

TO UNDERTAKE THE *EDUCATION* OF *FIVE DAUGHTERS* OF A *MRS. O'GALL* OF *CONNAUGHT*, *IRELAND*.

YOU'LL *LIKE* IRELAND, I THINK: THEY'RE SUCH *WARM-HEARTED PEOPLE* THERE, THEY *SAY*.

IT IS A *LONG WAY OFF*, SIR.

A *GIRL* OF *YOUR SENSE* WILL NOT OBJECT TO THE *VOYAGE* OR THE *DISTANCE*.

NOT THE *VOYAGE*, BUT THE *DISTANCE*: AND THEN THE *SEA* IS A *BARRIER* --

FROM *WHAT*, JANE?

-- FROM *ENGLAND* AND FROM *THORNFIELD*: AND --

-- FROM *YOU*, SIR.

WE HAVE BEEN *GOOD FRIENDS*, JANE; AND WHEN *FRIENDS* ARE ON THE *EVE* OF *SEPARATION*, THEY *LIKE* TO SPEND THE *LITTLE TIME* THAT *REMAINS* TO THEM *CLOSE* TO EACH OTHER.

I *SOMETIMES* HAVE A *QUEER* FEELING WITH *REGARD* TO YOU - *ESPECIALLY* WHEN YOU ARE *NEAR* ME, AS *NOW*:

IT IS AS IF I HAVE A *STRING* SOMEWHERE UNDER MY *LEFT RIBS*, TIGHTLY AND *INEXTRICABLY* KNOTTED TO A *SIMILAR* STRING SITUATED IN THE *CORRESPONDING QUARTER* OF *YOUR LITTLE FRAME*.

AND IF THAT **BOISTEROUS CHANNEL**, AND TWO HUNDRED **MILES** OR SO OF **LAND** COME **BROAD** BETWEEN US, I AM **AFRAID** THAT **CORD** OF **COMMUNION** WILL BE **SNAPPED**; AND THEN I'VE A NERVOUS **NOTION** I SHOULD **TAKE** TO BLEEDING INWARDLY.

AS FOR **YOU**, - YOU'D **FORGET** ME.

THAT I **NEVER** SHOULD, SIR.

JANE, DO YOU HEAR THAT **NIGHTINGALE** SINGING?

I **WISH** -SOB- I HAD -SOB- **NEVER COME** TO **THORNFIELD**.

I -SOB- **WISH** -SOB- I HAD **NEVER EVER** -SOB- BEEN **BORN**.

BECAUSE YOU ARE **SORRY** TO LEAVE IT?

I **GRIEVE** TO LEAVE THORNFIELD: I **LOVE** THORNFIELD, BECAUSE I HAVE **LIVED** IN IT A **FULL LIFE** AND HAVE NOT BEEN **TRAMPLED** ON.

I HAVE **TALKED** WITH AN **ORIGINAL**, EXPANDED MIND - YOU, MR. ROCHESTER.

I SEE THE **NECESSITY** OF **DEPARTURE**; AND IT IS LIKE **LOOKING** ON THE **NECESSITY** OF **DEATH**.

WHERE DO YOU SEE THE **NECESSITY**?

DO YOU **THINK** I CAN **STAY** TO BECOME **NOTHING** TO YOU? DO YOU **THINK** I AM A **MACHINE** WITHOUT **FEELINGS**? DO YOU THINK BECAUSE I AM **POOR** AND **PLAIN**, I AM **SOULLESS** AND **HEARTLESS**? I HAVE AS MUCH **SOUL** AS YOU - AND **FULL** AS MUCH **HEART**!

IT IS MY **SPIRIT** THAT ADDRESSES **YOUR** SPIRIT NOW --

-- JUST AS IF **BOTH** HAD **PASSED** THROUGH THE **GRAVE** AND **STOOD** AT **GOD'S FEET**, EQUAL - AS WE ARE!

AS WE **ARE**! SO - SO, JANE!

YET NOT SO, FOR **YOU** ARE **AS GOOD** AS MARRIED TO AN **INFERIOR** WHOM YOU **DO NOT LOVE**.

I **SCORN** SUCH A **UNION**: THEREFORE I AM **BETTER** THAN YOU --

-- LET ME GO!

JANE, DON'T **STRUGGLE** SO.

78

YOUR WILL SHALL **DECIDE** YOUR **DESTINY**. I OFFER YOU MY **HAND**, MY **HEART**, AND A **SHARE** OF ALL MY **POSSESSIONS**.

JANE, I **SUMMON** YOU AS MY **WIFE**. IT IS **YOU ONLY** I INTEND TO **MARRY**.

YOU PLAY A **FARCE**, WHICH I MERELY **LAUGH** AT. YOUR **BRIDE** STANDS BETWEEN US.

MY **BRIDE** IS **HERE**, BECAUSE MY **EQUAL** IS **HERE**, AND MY **LIKENESS**.

WHAT **LOVE** HAVE **I** FOR MISS INGRAM? **NONE**: AND **THAT** YOU KNOW.

WHAT **LOVE** HAS **SHE** FOR **ME**? **NONE**.

I **CAUSED** A **RUMOUR** TO REACH HER THAT MY **FORTUNE** WAS **FAR LESS** THAN SHE **THOUGHT**; AND SHE TURNED **COLD** TOWARDS ME. I **WOULD NOT** MARRY MISS INGRAM.

YOU **STRANGE**, ALMOST **UNEARTHLY THING**, I **LOVE YOU** AS MY **OWN FLESH**. I MUST **HAVE YOU** FOR MY **OWN** - ENTIRELY MY **OWN**.

JANE, WILL YOU **MARRY ME**?

MR. **ROCHESTER**, LET ME **LOOK** AT YOUR **FACE**.

TURN TO THE **MOONLIGHT**, BECAUSE I WANT TO **READ** YOUR COUNTENANCE.

MAKE **HASTE**, FOR I **SUFFER**.

DO YOU **SINCERELY** WISH ME TO BE YOUR **WIFE**?

I **DO**, I **SWEAR** IT.

THEN, SIR, I **WILL** MARRY YOU.

EDWARD --

-- MY **LITTLE WIFE**!

DEAR **EDWARD**!

KRAKK-OOOMM!!

GOD PARDON ME! AND MAN MEDDLE NOT WITH ME: I **HAVE HER**, AND WILL **HOLD HER**.

AGAIN AND **AGAIN**, HE SAID, "ARE YOU **HAPPY**, **JANE**?" AND AGAIN AND AGAIN I ANSWERED, "**YES**."

A BRILLIANT JUNE MORNING HAD **SUCCEEDED** TO THE **TEMPEST** OF THE **NIGHT**. I HASTENED TO **MEET** WITH **MR. ROCHESTER**.

WHY DID YOU TAKE SUCH **PAINS** TO MAKE ME **BELIEVE** YOU WISHED TO **MARRY MISS INGRAM?**

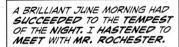

~ CHAPTER XXIV ~

ALTHOUGH I SHOULD MAKE YOU A LITTLE **INDIGNANT** - AND I HAVE **SEEN** WHAT A **FIRE-SPIRIT** YOU CAN BE - YOU **GLOWED** IN THE **COOL MOONLIGHT** LAST NIGHT, WHEN YOU **MUTINIED** AGAINST FATE, AND CLAIMED YOUR RANK AS MY EQUAL.

I FEIGNED COURTSHIP OF **MISS INGRAM** BECAUSE I WISHED TO **RENDER** YOU AS **MADLY** IN **LOVE** WITH ME AS **I WAS** WITH **YOU;** AND I KNEW **JEALOUSY** WOULD BE THE **BEST ALLY** I COULD CALL IN FOR THE **FURTHERANCE** OF THAT **END.**

DID YOU THINK **NOTHING** OF **MISS INGRAM'S** FEELINGS, SIR?

HER **FEELINGS** ARE CONCENTRATED IN **ONE - PRIDE;** AND **THAT** NEEDS **HUMBLING.**

YOU HAVE A **CURIOUS, DESIGNING** MIND, MR. ROCHESTER. I AM **AFRAID** YOUR **PRINCIPLES** ON **SOME** POINTS ARE **ECCENTRIC.**

I **LOVED** HIM **VERY MUCH** - MORE THAN **WORDS** HAD **POWER** TO **EXPRESS.**

MY **PRINCIPLES** WERE **NEVER TRAINED**, JANE; THEY **MAY** HAVE GROWN A LITTLE **AWRY** FOR **WANT** OF **ATTENTION.**

WE AGREED ON A **QUIET WEDDING**, BUT I FELT I SHOULD **WRITE** TO MY **UNCLE JOHN** IN MADEIRA TO **TELL** HIM ABOUT MY **MARRIAGE.**

~ CHAPTER XXV ~

THE **HURRY** OF PREPARATION FOR THE **BRIDAL DAY;** AND THE **ANTICIPATION** OF THE **GREAT CHANGE** MADE ME **FEVERISH.** ONE **NIGHT**, WHEN MR. ROCHESTER WAS **ABSENT** FROM **HOME**, MY **ANXIOUS EXCITEMENT** CONTINUED IN **DREAMS.**

THAT **SAME** NIGHT, I WOKE TO SEE A **GHOST** WEARING MY **WEDDING-DRESS** AND VEIL.

MY **BLOOD** CREPT **COLD** THROUGH MY **VEINS**. THE **SHAPE BEFORE ME** HAD **NEVER** CROSSED MY **EYES** BEFORE; THE **HEIGHT**, THE **CONTOUR** WERE **NEW** TO ME. IT WAS **NOT** EVEN THAT **STRANGE** WOMAN, **GRACE POOLE**.

I LOST **CONSCIOUSNESS** AND BECAME **INSENSIBLE** WITH **TERROR**.

THE **TRANSACTION** ACTUALLY **TOOK PLACE**. ON **RISING**, I SAW THE **VEIL** ON THE **CARPET**. IT WAS **TORN** FROM **TOP** TO **BOTTOM** AND IN **TWO HALVES**!

I **WAITED** NOW **MR. ROCHESTER'S RETURN**. I WAS **EAGER** TO **DISBURTHEN** MY **MIND**, AND TO **SEEK** OF HIM THE **SOLUTION** OF THE **ENIGMA** THAT **PERPLEXED ME**.

A WOMAN **DID**, I **DOUBT** NOT, ENTER YOUR ROOM: AND **THAT** WOMAN **MUST** HAVE BEEN **GRACE POOLE**. I **SEE** YOU WOULD **ASK** WHY I **KEEP** SUCH A WOMAN IN MY **HOUSE**:

WHEN WE HAVE BEEN **MARRIED** A YEAR AND A DAY, I WILL **TELL** YOU, BUT NOT **NOW**.

ARE YOU **SATISFIED**, JANE? DO YOU **ACCEPT** MY **SOLUTION** OF THE **MYSTERY**?

SATISFIED I WAS **NOT**, BUT TO **PLEASE** HIM I **ENDEAVOURED** TO BE SO - **RELIEVED**, I CERTAINLY **DID** FEEL.

MR. ROCHESTER **INSISTED** I **SLEEP** THAT NIGHT IN THE **NURSERY** WITH THE **DOOR BOLTED**. SOPHIE WAS TO **ROUSE** ME IN **GOOD** TIME FOR OUR **WEDDING** IN THE MORNING. WITH LITTLE **ADÈLE** IN MY ARMS, I WATCHED THE **SLUMBER** OF **CHILDHOOD** AND **WAITED** FOR THE **COMING DAY**; SHE SEEMED THE **EMBLEM** OF MY **PAST LIFE**.

~ CHAPTER XXVI ~

...WILT THOU **HAVE** THIS **WOMAN** FOR THY **WEDDED WIFE?**

THE MARRIAGE CANNOT **GO ON:** I DECLARE THE **EXISTENCE** OF AN **IMPEDIMENT.**

PROCEED.

I CANNOT **PROCEED** WITHOUT SOME **INVESTIGATION** - PERHAPS THIS IMPEDIMENT MAY BE **EXPLAINED AWAY?**

HARDLY! MR. ROCHESTER HAS A **WIFE** NOW **LIVING.**

FAVOUR ME WITH AN **ACCOUNT** OF HER.

MY NAME IS **BRIGGS** - A **SOLICITOR** OF **LONDON** - AND I HAVE A **WITNESS.**

MR. **MASON**, HAVE THE **GOODNESS** TO STEP **FORWARD.**

WHAT HAVE **YOU** TO SAY?

GOOD **GOD!**

THE **DEVIL** IS **IN IT** IF YOU CANNOT **ANSWER DISTINCTLY.**

SIR, DO NOT **FORGET** YOU ARE IN A **SACRED PLACE.**

COURAGE. SPEAK **OUT.**

SHE IS **NOW LIVING** AT **THORNFIELD HALL.** I **SAW** HER THERE LAST **APRIL.** I'M HER **BROTHER.**

NO, BY GOD!

ENOUGH! THERE WILL BE **NO WEDDING TO-DAY.** BIGAMY IS AN **UGLY WORD!** - I **MEANT**, HOWEVER, TO BE A **BIGAMIST;** BUT FATE HAS **OUT-MANOEUVRED** ME, OR **PROVIDENCE CHECKED** ME. I'M **LITTLE** BETTER THAN A **DEVIL** AT THIS **MOMENT;** AND **DESERVE,** NO **DOUBT,** THE **STERNEST** JUDGMENTS OF **GOD.**

A **LUNATIC** IS KEPT UNDER **WATCH** AT **THORNFIELD.** SHE IS MY **WIFE,** WHOM I **MARRIED FIFTEEN YEARS** AGO.

BERTHA MASON BY NAME; SISTER OF THIS **RESOLUTE PERSONAGE.**

CHEER UP, DICK! I'D **ALMOST** AS SOON **STRIKE A WOMAN** AS **YOU.**

BERTHA MASON IS **MAD;** AND SHE **CAME** OF A **MAD FAMILY;** IDIOTS AND MANIACS THROUGH **THREE GENERATIONS!** - AS I FOUND OUT **AFTER** I HAD WED THE **DAUGHTER.**

BERTHA, LIKE A **DUTIFUL CHILD,** COPIED HER **MOTHER** BY BEING A **MADWOMAN** AND A **DRUNKARD.**

OH, I WENT THROUGH **RICH SCENES!**

THIS *GIRL* KNEW *NO MORE* THAN *YOU* OF THE *DISGUSTING SECRET:* SHE *THOUGHT* ALL WAS *FAIR* AND *LEGAL,* AND NEVER *DREAMT* SHE WAS GOING TO BE *ENTRAPPED* INTO A *FEIGNED UNION* WITH A DEFRAUDED *WRETCH,* ALREADY *BOUND* TO A *BAD, MAD,* AND *EMBRUTED PARTNER!*

BRIGGS, WOOD, MASON, I INVITE YOU *ALL* TO COME UP TO THE HOUSE AND VISIT *MRS. POOLE'S* PATIENT, AND *MY WIFE!*

YOU SHALL *SEE* WHAT SORT OF *BEING* I WAS *CHEATED* INTO *ESPOUSING,* AND *JUDGE* WHETHER OR *NOT* I HAD A *RIGHT* TO *BREAK* THE *COMPACT,* AND SEEK *SYMPATHY* WITH *SOMETHING* AT *LEAST HUMAN.*

YOU KNOW THIS PLACE, *MASON* — SHE *BIT* AND *STABBED* YOU HERE.

GOOD MORNING, MRS. POOLE! HOW *ARE YOU* AND YOUR *CHARGE* TO-DAY?

WE'RE *TOLERABLE,* SIR, THANK YOU.

RATHER *SNAPPISH,* BUT NOT 'RAGEOUS.

YOU, MADAM, ARE **CLEARED** FROM **ALL BLAME**: YOUR **UNCLE** WILL BE **GLAD** TO **HEAR** IT - **IF**, INDEED, HE IS **STILL LIVING**.

MY UNCLE! DO YOU **KNOW** HIM?

THE **HOUSE CLEARED**. I **SHUT** MYSELF **IN** AND PROCEEDED - NOT TO WEEP, NOT TO **MOURN**, BUT - **MECHANICALLY** TO TAKE OFF THE WEDDING-DRESS, AND REPLACE IT BY THE GOWN I WORE YESTERDAY; YET WHERE WAS THE JANE EYRE OF **YESTERDAY**? **WHERE** WAS HER **LIFE**? **WHERE** WERE HER **PROSPECTS**? I SANK IN DEEP MIRE; THE FLOODS OVERFLOWED ME.

WELL, JANE! NO WORD OF REPROACH? NOTHING **BITTER**? I NEVER **MEANT** TO WOUND YOU THUS!

WILL YOU **EVER FORGIVE** ME?

~ CHAPTER ~
~ XXVII ~

I **FORGAVE HIM** AT THE **MOMENT** AND ON THE **SPOT**. THERE WAS SUCH DEEP REMORSE IN HIS EYE, SUCH **UNCHANGED LOVE** IN HIS **WHOLE LOOK**. I **FORGAVE** HIM **ALL**: YET **NOT IN WORDS**, NOT **OUTWARDLY**; ONLY AT MY **HEART'S CORE**.

MR. **MASON** WAS **WITH HIM** AT **MADEIRA** WHEN HE RECEIVED YOUR **LETTER** INTIMATING THE **CONTEMPLATED UNION**.

MR. **MASON REVEALED** THE **REAL STATE OF MATTERS**.

YOUR **UNCLE** IS NOW ON A **SICK-BED**, BUT **IMPLORED** MR. **MASON** TO PREVENT THE **FALSE MARRIAGE**.

YOU **KNOW** I AM A **SCOUNDREL, JANE?**

YES, SIR.

THEN **TELL ME** SO **ROUNDLY, SHARPLY**.

I **CANNOT**: I AM **TIRED** AND **SICK**.

IF I COULD **GO OUT OF** LIFE NOW, IT WOULD BE **WELL** FOR ME. THEN I SHOULD NOT HAVE TO **CRACK MY HEART-STRINGS** IN RENDING THEM FROM MR. ROCHESTER'S. I **MUST** LEAVE HIM. I **DO NOT WANT** TO LEAVE HIM. I **CANNOT** LEAVE HIM.

YOU **INTEND** TO **MAKE** YOURSELF A COMPLETE **STRANGER** TO ME.

ALL IS **CHANGED** ABOUT ME, SIR: I MUST CHANGE **TOO**.

ADÈLE MUST HAVE A **NEW GOVERNESS**, SIR.

ADÈLE WILL GO TO **SCHOOL** - I HAVE **SETTLED** THAT **ALREADY**.

I WAS **WRONG** TO **BRING** YOU HERE. I FEARED A GOVERNESS WOULD NEVER **STAY** IF SHE HAD KNOWLEDGE OF THE **CURSE**; AND MY **PLANS** WOULD NOT **PERMIT** ME TO REMOVE THE **MANIAC ELSEWHERE** --

...THOUGH I **POSSESS** AN **OLD HOUSE, FERNDEAN MANOR**, WHERE I **COULD** HAVE LODGED HER. **PROBABLY** THOSE **DAMP WALLS** WOULD HAVE SOON **EASED** ME OF HER **CHARGE**. MY **CONSCIENCE RECOILED** FROM THE **ARRANGEMENT**.

I'LL **SHUT UP THORNFIELD HALL**: I'LL GIVE MRS. POOLE TWO HUNDRED A YEAR TO BE AT HAND WHEN MY **WIFE** IS **PROMPTED** BY HER **FAMILIAR** TO BURN PEOPLE IN THEIR BEDS, **STAB** AND **BITE** THEIR FLESH, AND **SO ON**...

SIR, YOU SPEAK OF HER WITH HATE.

IT IS CRUEL - SHE CANNOT HELP BEING MAD.

JANE, MY LITTLE DARLING, YOU MISJUDGE ME AGAIN:

IT IS NOT BECAUSE SHE IS MAD I HATE HER. IF YOU WERE MAD, DO YOU THINK I SHOULD HATE YOU?

I DO INDEED, SIR.

THEN YOU ARE MISTAKEN, AND YOU KNOW NOTHING ABOUT ME AND NOTHING ABOUT THE SORT OF LOVE OF WHICH I AM CAPABLE.

EVERY ATOM OF YOUR FLESH IS AS DEAR TO ME AS MY OWN. I SHOULD NOT SHRINK FROM YOU WITH DISGUST AS I DID FROM HER.

I COULD NEVER WEARY OF GAZING INTO YOUR EYES, THOUGH THEY HAD NO LONGER A RAY OF RECOGNITION FOR ME.

JANE! JANE! YOU DON'T LOVE ME, THEN?

I DO LOVE YOU - MORE THAN EVER: BUT I MUST NOT SHOW OR INDULGE THE FEELING;

AND THIS IS THE LAST TIME I MUST EXPRESS IT --

-- AND THEREFORE, MR. ROCHESTER, I MUST LEAVE YOU.

FOR HOW LONG, JANE?

I MUST PART WITH YOU FOR MY WHOLE LIFE: I MUST BEGIN A NEW EXISTENCE.

OF COURSE. I PASS OVER THE MADNESS ABOUT PARTING FROM ME.

I AM NOT MARRIED.

YOU SHALL BE MRS. ROCHESTER AND LIVE IN A VILLA I HAVE IN THE SOUTH OF FRANCE.

SIR, YOUR WIFE IS LIVING: THAT IS A FACT ACKNOWLEDGED THIS MORNING BY YOURSELF.

IF I LIVED WITH YOU AS YOU DESIRE - I SHOULD THEN BE YOUR MISTRESS: TO SAY OTHERWISE IS SOPHISTICAL - IS FALSE.

JANE, I AM NOT A GENTLE-TEMPERED MAN - BEWARE!

WILL YOU HEAR REASON? BECAUSE, IF YOU WON'T, I'LL TRY VIOLENCE.

I SAW THAT ONE PASSING SECOND OF TIME WAS ALL I HAD TO RESTRAIN HIM. I WAS NOT AFRAID; I FELT AN INWARD POWER, A SENSE OF INFLUENCE, WHICH SUPPORTED ME.

SIT DOWN; I'LL TALK TO YOU AS LONG AS YOU LIKE, AND HEAR ALL YOU HAVE TO SAY.

I AM NOT ANGRY, JANE: I ONLY LOVE YOU TOO WELL;

AND YOU HAD STEELED YOUR LITTLE PALE FACE WITH SUCH A RESOLUTE, FROZEN LOOK, I COULD NOT ENDURE IT.

HUSH NOW.

JUST PUT YOUR HAND IN MINE, AND I WILL SHOW YOU THE REAL STATE OF THE CASE. CAN YOU LISTEN TO ME?

YES SIR; FOR HOURS, IF YOU WILL.

MY FATHER WAS AN AVARICIOUS, GRASPING MAN WHO COULD NOT BEAR THE IDEA OF DIVIDING HIS ESTATE: ALL, HE RESOLVED, SHOULD GO TO MY BROTHER, ROWLAND.

YET AS LITTLE COULD HE ENDURE THAT A SON OF HIS SHOULD BE A POOR MAN.

NOW THAT YOU HAVE LEFT COLLEGE, EDWARD, YOU MUST GO TO A BUSINESS PARTNER I'VE FOUND FOR YOU - A PLANTER AND MERCHANT IN JAMAICA.

HIS DAUGHTER BERTHA IS THE BOAST OF SPANISH TOWN FOR HER BEAUTY.

THIS WAS NO LIE; THOUGH MY FATHER SAID NOTHING ABOUT BERTHA MASON'S FORTUNE OF THIRTY THOUSAND POUNDS. MY BRIDE HAD ALREADY BEEN COURTED FOR ME.

87

HER *FAMILY* WISHED TO *SECURE ME*, BECAUSE I WAS OF A *GOOD RACE*; AND *SO DID SHE*. THEY *SHOWED HER* TO ME IN *PARTIES*, SPLENDIDLY DRESSED. I WAS DAZZLED: I *THOUGHT* I *LOVED* HER.

COMPETITORS *PIQUED* ME: SHE *ALLURED* ME: A *MARRIAGE* WAS ACHIEVED ALMOST *BEFORE* I *KNEW* WHERE I *WAS*. I DID NOT EVEN *KNOW* HER.

THE HONEYMOON *OVER*, I *LEARNED* MY *MISTAKE*; MY *BRIDE'S MOTHER* WAS *SHUT UP* IN A *LUNATIC ASYLUM*, AND THERE WAS A *YOUNGER, DUMB IDIOT*, OF A *BROTHER*.

MY *FATHER* AND *BROTHER KNEW* ALL THIS; BUT THEY *ONLY THOUGHT* OF THE *MONEY*, AND *JOINED IN* THE *PLOT AGAINST* ME.

I LIVED WITH THAT WOMAN *FOUR YEARS*, AND *BEFORE* THAT TIME SHE HAD *TRIED ME INDEED*. I COULD NOT PASS A *SINGLE HOUR* WITH HER IN *COMFORT*. NO *SERVANT* WOULD BEAR THE OUTBREAKS OF HER *VIOLENCE* AND *UNREASONABLE TEMPER*. I COULD NOT LEGALLY *RID* MYSELF OF HER FOR THE *DOCTORS* DECLARED HER AS *MAD*.

BOOOMMM!!!

THIS *LIFE* IS *HELL* - I HAVE A *RIGHT* TO *DELIVER MYSELF* FROM IT.

LET ME *BREAK AWAY*, AND *GO HOME* TO GOD!

F@!? EDWARD ROCHESTER!

?!£!

?!?@!!!

EDWARD! $*?!

I ONLY *ENTERTAINED* THE *INTENTION* FOR A *MOMENT*.

AS I *WALKED* IN MY *WET GARDEN*, I SAW *HOPE REVIVE* - AND FELT *REGENERATION* POSSIBLE. "*RETURN TO EUROPE!*" SAID HOPE. "*YOUR FILTHY BURDEN* IS *NOT KNOWN* THERE. *SHELTER* HER *DEGRADATION* WITH *SECRECY*; AND *LEAVE HER*." MY *FATHER*, ANXIOUS TO *CONCEAL* THE *CONNECTION*, HELPED ME TO *HIDE* HER AT *THORNFIELD HALL*.

MY *BROTHER* IN THE *INTERVAL* WAS *DEAD*, AND MY *FATHER* SOON DIED *TOO*.

FOR *TEN LONG YEARS* I ROVE ABOUT. WITH *PLENTY* OF MONEY, I COULD CHOOSE MY OWN *SOCIETY*. NO *CIRCLES* WERE CLOSED *AGAINST* ME. AROUND THE *CITIES* OF EUROPE, I SOUGHT *HER* WHO *SUITED* ME.

WELL, SIR? DID YOU **FIND** ANYONE YOU **LIKED?**

THE **FIRST** I CHOSE WAS **CÉLINE VARENS** - YOU **ALREADY** KNOW HOW **THAT** LIAISON TERMINATED.

SHE HAD **TWO** SUCCESSORS.

I DID **NOT** - YET I **COULD** NOT LIVE **ALONE;**

HIRING A **MISTRESS** IS THE **NEXT WORSE THING** TO BUYING A **SLAVE:**

BOTH ARE OFTEN BY **NATURE**, AND **ALWAYS** BY **POSITION**, INFERIOR: AND TO LIVE **FAMILIARLY** WITH **INFERIORS** IS DEGRADING.

SO I **TRIED** THE COMPANIONSHIP OF **MISTRESSES.**

I **DREW** FROM THESE **WORDS** THAT WERE **I** TO BE THEIR **SUCCESSOR**, HE WOULD **ONE** DAY **REGARD ME** WITH THE **SAME FEELING.**

LAST **JANUARY**, **RID** OF ALL MY **MISTRESSES**, I **RETURNED** TO ENGLAND, **SOURLY DISPOSED** AGAINST **ALL WOMANKIND.**

RIDING ON A **FROSTY WINTER AFTERNOON**, I SAW A QUIET **LITTLE FIGURE** SITTING BY **ITSELF;** AND ON THE **OCCASION** OF MY **HORSE'S ACCIDENT**, IT **CAME UP** AND GRAVELY OFFERED ME **HELP.**

IT **SEEMED** AS IF A **LINNET** HAD **HOPPED** TO MY **FOOT** AND PROPOSED TO **BEAR ME** ON ITS TINY **WING.**

I WAS **SURLY;** BUT THE THING **WOULD NOT GO:** IT STOOD **BY** ME WITH **STRANGE PERSEVERANCE**, AND SPOKE WITH A SORT OF **AUTHORITY:** I **MUST BE AIDED**, AND BY THAT **HAND:** AND **AIDED I WAS.** WHEN **ONCE** I HAD PRESSED THE **FRAIL SHOULDER**, SOMETHING **NEW** STOLE INTO MY **FRAME.**

YOU **SEE NOW** HOW THE **CASE STANDS** - DO YOU **NOT?** I **HAVE** FOR THE FIRST TIME **FOUND** WHAT I CAN **TRULY LOVE** - I HAVE **FOUND YOU.**

YOU **UNDERSTAND** WHAT I **WANT** OF YOU? JUST THIS **PROMISE** - "I WILL BE YOURS, **MR. ROCHESTER.**"

MR. **ROCHESTER**, I WILL **NOT** BE **YOURS.**

JANE, DO YOU *MEAN* TO GO *ONE* WAY IN THE WORLD, AND TO LET *ME* GO *ANOTHER?*

I *DO.*

OH, *JANE,* THIS IS *BITTER!* THIS - THIS IS *WICKED.* IT WOULD *NOT* BE WICKED TO *LOVE* ME.

IT *WOULD* TO *OBEY* YOU.

WHAT SHALL I *DO,* JANE? WHERE *TURN* FOR A *COMPANION,* AND FOR SOME *HOPE?*

DO AS *I* DO: TRUST IN *GOD,* AND *YOURSELF.* BELIEVE IN *HEAVEN.* HOPE TO *MEET AGAIN* THERE.

YOU *CONDEMN* ME TO *LIVE WRETCHED,* AND TO *DIE ACCURSED.*

I *ADVISE* YOU TO *LIVE SINLESS,* AND I *WISH* YOU TO *DIE TRANQUIL.*

NEVER WAS *ANYTHING* AT ONCE SO *FRAIL* AND SO *INDOMITABLE.*

WHATEVER I DO WITH ITS *CAGE,* I *CANNOT GET AT IT* - IF I *TEAR,* IF I *REND* THE *SLIGHT PRISON,* MY *OUTRAGE* WILL ONLY LET THE CAPTIVE *LOOSE.*

CONQUEROR I MIGHT BE OF THE *HOUSE,* BUT THE *INMATE* WOULD ESCAPE TO *HEAVEN* BEFORE I COULD CALL MYSELF *POSSESSOR* OF ITS *CLAY DWELLING PLACE.*

AND IT IS *YOU,* SPIRIT - WITH *WILL* AND *ENERGY, VIRTUE* AND *PURITY* - THAT I *WANT:* NOT *ALONE* YOUR *BRITTLE FRAME.*

OF YOURSELF YOU COULD *COME* WITH *SOFT FLIGHT* AND *NESTLE* AGAINST MY *HEART.*

SEIZED AGAINST YOUR *WILL,* YOU WILL *ELUDE* THE *GRASP* LIKE AN *ESSENCE* - YOU WILL *VANISH* ERE I *INHALE* YOUR *FRAGRANCE.*

I AM **GOING**, SIR.

YOU ARE **LEAVING** ME?

YES. **GOD BLESS** YOU, MY **DEAR MASTER**!

AND **KEEP** YOU FROM **HARM** AND **WRONG** - **DIRECT** YOU, **SOLACE** YOU - **REWARD** YOU **WELL** FOR YOUR **PAST KINDNESS** TO ME. **FAREWELL**!

OH, **JANE**! MY **HOPE** - MY **LOVE** - MY **LIFE**!

I **ROSE** AT **DAWN** TO LEAVE THORNFIELD HALL. IN MR. **ROCHESTER'S** CHAMBER, THE **INMATE** WAS **WALKING RESTLESSLY** FROM **WALL** TO **WALL**. I **KNEW** WHAT I HAD TO **DO**, AND DID IT **MECHANICALLY**.

I WAS **OUT** OF **THORNFIELD**. THERE LAY A **ROAD** WHICH **STRETCHED** IN THE **CONTRARY** DIRECTION TO **MILLCOTE**; THITHER I BENT MY **STEPS**.

I **THOUGHT** OF HIM NOW, IN HIS **ROOM**, HOPING I SHOULD SOON COME TO **SAY** I WOULD BE **HIS**. I **LONGED** TO BE **HIS**; IT WAS NOT **TOO LATE**. I **COULD** GO **BACK** AND BE HIS **REDEEMER**. BIRDS WERE **FAITHFUL** TO THEIR **MATES**; **BIRDS** WERE **EMBLEMS** OF **LOVE**. WHAT WAS **I**? I HAD **INJURED** - **WOUNDED** - **LEFT** MY **MASTER**. I WAS **HATEFUL** IN MY **OWN EYES**. STILL I **COULD NOT** TURN, NOR **RETRACE** ONE STEP.

I WAS **WEEPING WILDLY** AS I **WALKED**: FAST, FAST I WENT LIKE ONE **DELIRIOUS**.

WHERE ARE YOU **GOING**?

WHITCROSS - FOR **THIRTY SHILLINGS**, MISS.

I **ONLY** HAVE **TWENTY**.

WELL, I WILL **TRY** TO **MAKE** IT **DO**. GET **INSIDE**.

MAY **NO-ONE** EVER **FEEL** WHAT I **THEN FELT**! TO BE THE **INSTRUMENT** OF **EVIL** TO WHAT THEY **WHOLLY LOVE**.

~ CHAPTER ~
~ XXVIII ~

AFTER **TWO DAYS**, THE **COACHMAN** SET ME **DOWN** AT **WHITCROSS**. IT IS NO **TOWN**; BUT A **STONE PILLAR** SET UP WHERE **FOUR ROADS** MEET.

WHEN THE **COACH** WAS A **MILE OFF**, I DISCOVERED THAT MY **PARCEL** REMAINED ON THE **COACH**. I WAS **ALONE** AND **DESTITUTE**. NOT A **TIE** HELD ME TO **HUMAN** SOCIETY. I HAD NO **RELATIVE** BUT THE **UNIVERSAL** MOTHER, **NATURE**.

NATURE SEEMED TO ME **BENIGN** AND **GOOD**; I THOUGHT SHE **LOVED** ME, **OUTCAST** AS I **WAS**; AND I, WHO FROM **MAN** COULD ANTICIPATE ONLY **MISTRUST**, **REJECTION**, **INSULT**, CLUNG TO HER WITH **FILIAL FONDNESS**.

TO-NIGHT, AT **LEAST**, I WOULD BE HER **GUEST**, AS I WAS HER **CHILD**. MY **REST** MIGHT HAVE BEEN **BLISSFUL** ENOUGH, ONLY A **SAD HEART BROKE** IT. IT **TREMBLED** FOR MR. ROCHESTER AND HIS **DOOM**; IT **DEMANDED** HIM WITH **CEASELESS LONGING**.

WE **KNOW** THAT **GOD** IS **EVERYWHERE**; WE **FEEL** HIS **PRESENCE MOST** WHEN HIS **WORKS** ARE ON THE **GRANDEST SCALE** SPREAD **BEFORE** US.

MR. **ROCHESTER** WAS **SAFE**: HE WAS **GOD'S**, AND BY **GOD** WOULD HE BE **GUARDED**.

BUT NEXT DAY, **WANT** CAME TO ME, PALE AND BARE. I TURNED TOWARDS A **CHURCH BELL** AND CAME ACROSS A NEARBY **HAMLET. THERE** I SOUGHT **EMPLOYMENT** BUT **FOUND NONE**. I SOUGHT **FOOD**, AND SHAMEFULLY OFFERED MY **POSSESSIONS** IN EXCHANGE - BUT WAS **REFUSED**.

ALL **DAY** I **BEGGED** AND **PRAYED** FOR PROVIDENCE.

DECIDING I WOULD RATHER **DIE** IN THE **LANDSCAPE** THAN IN THE **STREET**, I TURNED TOWARDS A **HILL**. AS NIGHT APPROACHED, I FOUND MYSELF **WALKING**, **EXHAUSTED**, TOWARDS A **DISTANT LIGHT**.

THIS **LIGHT** WAS MY **FORLORN HOPE**: I MUST **GAIN** IT.

I NEED A **NIGHT'S SHELTER** IN AN **OUTHOUSE** OR **ANYWHERE**, AND A **MORSEL** OF **BREAD** TO EAT.

I'LL GIVE YOU A PIECE OF **BREAD**, BUT WE **CAN'T** TAKE IN A **VAGRANT**.

BUT I MUST **DIE** IF I'M **TURNED AWAY**.

NOT YOU. I'M **FEAR'D** YOU HAVE SOME **ILL PLANS** AGATE, THAT **BRING** YOU ABOUT **FOLK'S HOUSES** AT **THIS** TIME O' NIGHT. WE HAVE A **GENTLEMAN** IN THE HOUSE, AND **DOGS**, AND **GUNS**.

I CAN BUT **DIE**, AND I **BELIEVE** IN **GOD**. LET ME **TRY** TO **WAIT** HIS **WILL** IN **SILENCE**.

ALL MEN MUST **DIE**. BUT **ALL** ARE **NOT** CONDEMNED TO MEET A **LINGERING**, PREMATURE **DOOM**, SUCH AS **YOURS** WOULD BE IF YOU **PERISHED** HERE OF **WANT**.

WHO OR **WHAT** SPEAKS?

IS IT **YOU**, MR. **ST. JOHN**? YOUR **SISTERS** ARE QUITE UNEASY. **BAD FOLKS** ARE **ABOUT**. A BEGGAR-WOMAN —

— I DECLARE, SHE IS **NOT GONE** YET!

MOVE OFF, I SAY!

HUSH, HANNAH! YOU HAVE **DONE** YOUR **DUTY** IN **EXCLUDING**, LET ME DO MINE IN **ADMITTING** HER. THIS IS A **PECULIAR CASE**.

THE **RECOLLECTION** OF ABOUT **THREE DAYS** AND **NIGHTS SUCCEEDING** THIS ARE VERY **DIM** IN MY **MIND**. THEY GAVE ME **FOOD**; I THEN LAY **MOTIONLESS** ON A **NARROW BED** IN A **SMALL ROOM**.

IT IS **VERY WELL** WE **TOOK** HER IN.

YES; SHE WOULD **CERTAINLY** HAVE BEEN FOUND **DEAD** AT THE **DOOR** IN THE **MORNING**. SHE IS NOT AN **UNEDUCATED** PERSON.

~ CHAPTER XXIX ~

ON THE **FIFTH DAY**, I WAS **WELL** ENOUGH TO GET UP. I TOLD THEM MY **NAME** WAS **JANE ELLIOTT**.

I **TRUST** I SHALL NOT **EAT** LONG AT YOUR **EXPENSE**.

NO, WHEN YOU TELL MY **SISTERS**, **DIANA** AND **MARY**, AND I YOUR **RESIDENCE**.

THAT IS **OUT** OF MY **POWER** TO DO, BEING **ABSOLUTELY** WITHOUT **HOME** AND **FRIENDS**.

A MOST **SINGULAR** POSITION AT **YOUR AGE**! YOU ARE A **SPINSTER**?

SHE **CAN'T** BE ABOVE **EIGHTEEN**, ST. JOHN.

I AM **NEAR NINETEEN**: BUT I AM **NOT MARRIED.**

WHERE DID YOU LAST **RESIDE?**

THAT IS MY SECRET.

MR. RIVERS, **YOU** AND YOUR **SISTERS** HAVE **RESCUED** ME FROM **DEATH.** THIS GIVES YOU AN **UNLIMITED CLAIM** ON MY **GRATITUDE,** AND A **CLAIM,** TO A **CERTAIN** EXTENT, ON MY **CONFIDENCE.**

WHICH YOU HAVE A **RIGHT** TO **KEEP** BOTH FROM **ST. JOHN** AND **EVERY OTHER** QUESTIONER.

YET IF I KNOW NOTHING **ABOUT** YOU OR YOUR **HISTORY,** I CANNOT **HELP** YOU. AND YOU **NEED** HELP, DO YOU **NOT?**

I **TOLD** THEM MY **STORY,** **APART** FROM THE **NAMES** AND **SITUATIONS** INVOLVING MY **RELATIONS** WITH **MR. ROCHESTER.**

I HAVE **HEARD** OF MR. **BROCKLEHURST,** AND **LOWOOD SCHOOL.**

YOU **SAID** YOUR **NAME** WAS **JANE ELLIOTT?**

I **DID** SAY SO; BUT IT IS **NOT** MY **REAL NAME. THAT** I WILL NOT **GIVE** FOR **FEAR** OF **DISCOVERY.**

MY **SISTERS** DERIVE **PLEASURE** FROM **KEEPING** YOU - AS THEY **WOULD** IN KEEPING A **HALF-FROZEN BIRD.**

I FEEL **MORE** INCLINATION TO PUT YOU IN THE **WAY** OF **KEEPING YOURSELF;** BUT MY **AID** MUST BE THE **HUMBLEST SORT.**

SHE HAS ALREADY **SAID** THAT SHE IS **WILLING** TO DO **ANYTHING HONEST** SHE CAN **DO.** SHE IS **FORCED,** ST. JOHN, TO PUT UP WITH SUCH **CRUSTY PEOPLE** AS YOU!

CHAPTER XXX

WHILE MY *HEALTH* RECOVERED, I JOINED *DIANA* AND *MARY* IN ALL THEIR *OCCUPATIONS* AND FOUND *BETWEEN* US A PERFECT *CONGENIALITY* OF *TASTES*, *SENTIMENTS*, AND *PRINCIPLES*; AND A *CHARM* BOTH *POTENT* AND *PERMANENT* IN THEIR *SEQUESTERED* HOME IN THE *PURPLE MOORS*.

THEY WERE BOTH *MORE ACCOMPLISHED* AND *BETTER READ* THAN I WAS. I *DEVOURED* THE *BOOKS* THEY LENT ME; *THEN* IT WAS *FULL SATISFACTION* TO *DISCUSS* WITH THEM IN THE EVENING WHAT I HAD *PERUSED* DURING THE *DAY*.

THOUGHT FITTED THOUGHT, *OPINION* MET OPINION. WE *COINCIDED*, IN *SHORT*, PERFECTLY.

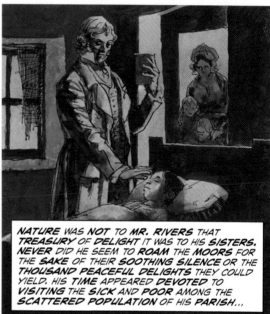

NATURE WAS *NOT* TO *MR. RIVERS* THAT *TREASURY* OF *DELIGHT* IT WAS TO HIS *SISTERS*. *NEVER* DID HE SEEM TO *ROAM* THE *MOORS* FOR THE *SAKE* OF THEIR *SOOTHING SILENCE* OR THE *THOUSAND PEACEFUL DELIGHTS* THEY COULD YIELD. HIS *TIME* APPEARED *DEVOTED* TO *VISITING* THE *SICK* AND *POOR* AMONG THE *SCATTERED POPULATION* OF HIS *PARISH*...

...AND *PREACHING* IN HIS *OWN CHURCH*. WHEN HE HAD *FINISHED*, INSTEAD OF FEELING *BETTER*, I EXPERIENCED *SADNESS*. HE HAD NO MORE FOUND 'THE *PEACE* OF GOD WHICH PASSETH ALL *UNDERSTANDING*' THAN HAD I CONCEALED MY *REGRETS* FOR MY *BROKEN IDOL* AND *LOST ELYSIUM*.

MARY AND *DIANA* WILL SOON *LEAVE* MOOR HOUSE, AND *RETURN* AS *GOVERNESSES* TO *HAUGHTY FAMILIES* WHO NEITHER *KNOW* NOR *SEEK* THEIR *INNATE EXCELLENCES*, APPRECIATING THEM *ONLY* AS THEY APPRECIATE THE *SKILL* OF THEIR *COOK* OR THE *TASTE* OF THEIR *WAITING-WOMAN*.

MR. ST. JOHN HAD SAID NOTHING TO ME YET ABOUT THE EMPLOYMENT HE HAD PROMISED TO OBTAIN FOR ME. ONE MORNING, WE WERE ALONE IN THE PARLOUR...

I BELIEVE YOU WILL ACCEPT THE POST I OFFER YOU.

I MEAN TO OPEN A SCHOOL FOR GIRLS - WILL YOU BE ITS MISTRESS?

I THANK YOU FOR THE PROPOSAL, MR. RIVERS --

-- AND I ACCEPT IT WITH ALL MY HEART.

IT IS A VILLAGE SCHOOL, WITH A HOUSE KINDLY PROVIDED BY A RICH HEIRESS, MISS OLIVER.

YOUR SCHOLARS WILL BE ONLY POOR GIRLS. KNITTING, SEWING, READING, WRITING, CIPHERING, WILL BE ALL YOU WILL HAVE TO TEACH.

WHAT WILL YOU DO WITH YOUR ACCOMPLISHMENTS?

SAVE THEM TILL THEY ARE WANTED. THEY WILL KEEP. I WILL OPEN THE SCHOOL NEXT WEEK, IF YOU LIKE.

VERY WELL: SO BE IT.

YOU WILL NOT STAY LONG; I READ IT IN YOUR EYE.

I AM NOT AMBITIOUS.

WELL IF YOU ARE NOT AMBITIOUS, YOU ARE --

-- IMPASSIONED...

...HUMAN AFFECTION AND SYMPATHIES HAVE A MOST POWERFUL HOLD ON YOU. I AM SURE YOU CANNOT DEVOTE YOUR WORKING HOURS TO A MONOTONOUS LABOUR WHOLLY VOID OF STIMULUS, ANY MORE THAN I.

A MISSIONARY I RESOLVE TO BE.

YOU HEAR NOW HOW I CONTRADICT MYSELF. I, WHO PREACH CONTENTMENT WITH A HUMBLE LOT, ALMOST RAVE IN MY RESTLESSNESS.

IN THIS BRIEF HOUR I HAD LEARNT MORE OF HIM THAN IN THE WHOLE PREVIOUS MONTH: YET STILL HE PUZZLED ME.

ST. JOHN WILL SACRIFICE **ALL** TO HIS **LONG-FRAMED** RESOLVES. HE **LOOKS** QUIET, JANE; BUT HE **HIDES** A FEVER IN HIS **VITALS**. YOU WOULD **THINK** HIM GENTLE, YET IN **SOME** THINGS HE IS INEXORABLE AS DEATH.

IT IS **RIGHT**, NOBLE, CHRISTIAN: YET IT **BREAKS** MY **HEART**!

WE ARE NOW WITHOUT **FATHER**. WE SHALL **SOON** BE WITHOUT **HOME** AND **BROTHER**.

AT **THAT** MOMENT A LITTLE ACCIDENT SUPERVENED, WHICH **SEEMED** TO PROVE THAT **MISFORTUNES** NEVER COME **SINGLY**.

OUR UNCLE JOHN IS **DEAD**.

AND WHAT **THEN**?

WHAT **THEN**? WHY - NOTHING.

READ.

AT **ANY** RATE, IT MAKES US NO **WORSE** OFF THAN WE WERE **BEFORE**.

WE HAVE **NEVER SEEN** OUR **UNCLE**.

LONG **AGO**, HE GAVE MY **FATHER** SOME **BAD BUSINESS** ADVICE WHICH **RUINED HIM**.

AFTERWARDS, MY **UNCLE** REALISED A **FORTUNE** AND MY **FATHER** CHERISHED THE **IDEA** THAT HE WOULD **ATONE** BY LEAVING HIS **POSSESSIONS** TO US.

HE HAS **NOT**.

WE WOULD HAVE **ESTEEMED** OURSELVES **RICH**, AND IT **WOULD** HAVE ENABLED **ST. JOHN** TO DO **MUCH GOOD**.

IN A **WEEK**, THE **OLD GRANGE** WAS **ABANDONED**. THE **VILLAGE SCHOOL** OPENED WITH **TWENTY SCHOLARS**. SOME WERE **UNMANNERED, ROUGH, INTRACTABLE**, AS WELL AS **IGNORANT**; BUT OTHERS WERE **DOCILE**; HAD A **WISH** TO **LEARN**, AND **PLEASING DISPOSITIONS**.

~ CHAPTER XXXI ~

BUT **THREE** OF THE **NUMBER** CAN **READ**: NONE WRITE OR **CIPHER**. SEVERAL **KNIT**, AND A FEW **SEW** A LITTLE.

WHICH IS **BETTER**? TO HAVE **SURRENDERED** TO TEMPTATION; LISTENED TO PASSION; - BUT TO HAVE **SUNK DOWN** IN THE **SILKEN SNARE**, FEVERED WITH **DELUSIVE BLISS** ONE HOUR, SUFFOCATING WITH **TEARS** OF **REMORSE** AND **SHAME** THE NEXT?

OR TO BE A **VILLAGE SCHOOL-MISTRESS**, **FREE** AND **HONEST**, IN A **BREEZY NOOK** IN THE **HEALTHY HEART** OF **ENGLAND**?

THE **BIRDS** SANG THEIR **LAST STRAINS** OF THE **DAY**. I THOUGHT MYSELF **HAPPY**, AND WAS **SURPRISED** TO FIND MYSELF ERE **LONG** WEEPING FOR WHAT I HAD **LEFT BEHIND**.

I **CANNOT STAY**. I HAVE ONLY BROUGHT YOU A LITTLE **PARCEL** MY **SISTERS** LEFT FOR YOU.

I **THINK** IT CONTAINS A **COLOUR-BOX**, **PENCILS**, AND **PAPER**.

A **WELCOME GIFT**.

DO YOU FIND **SOLITUDE** AN **OPPRESSION**?

I HAVE **HARDLY** HAD **TIME** YET TO ENJOY A SENSE OF **TRANQUILLITY**, MUCH LESS **LONELINESS**.

IT IS **HARD WORK** TO **CONTROL** THE WORKINGS OF **INCLINATION** AND **TURN** THE **BENT** OF NATURE; BUT THAT IT **MAY BE DONE**, I KNOW FROM **EXPERIENCE**.

GOOD-EVENING, MR. RIVERS. YOUR **DOG** IS **QUICKER** TO **RECOGNISE** HIS **FRIENDS** THAN YOU ARE, SIR.

THIS THEN, I THOUGHT, IS **MISS ROSAMOND OLIVER**, THE **HEIRESS**.

A **LOVELY** EVENING, BUT **LATE** FOR YOU TO BE **OUT ALONE**.

PAPA TOLD ME YOU HAD **OPENED** YOUR **SCHOOL**, AND THAT THE NEW **MISTRESS** WAS COME; **THIS IS SHE**?

IT **IS**.

I SHALL **COME UP** AND HELP TEACH SOMETIMES. IT WILL BE A **CHANGE** FOR ME TO **VISIT** NOW AND AGAIN; AND I **LIKE** A **CHANGE**.

PAPA SAYS YOU NEVER COME TO **SEE US** NOW. YOU ARE **QUITE** A **STRANGER** AT **VALE HALL**.

DO COME AND SEE **PAPA**.

NOT **TO-NIGHT**, MISS ROSAMOND.

SHE WENT **ONE WAY**; HE **ANOTHER**.

THIS **SPECTACLE** OF **ANOTHER'S** SUFFERING AND **SACRIFICE** RAPT MY **THOUGHTS** FROM **EXCLUSIVE MEDITATION** ON MY **OWN**. DIANA RIVERS HAD DESIGNATED HER BROTHER "**INEXORABLE AS DEATH**". SHE HAD **NOT EXAGGERATED**.

I FELT I BECAME A *FAVOURITE* IN THE NEIGHBOURHOOD. TO *LIVE* AMIDST *GENERAL REGARD* IS LIKE 'SITTING IN SUNSHINE, CALM AND *SWEET*'; SERENE INWARD FEELINGS BUD AND BLOOM UNDER THE *RAY*. AT THIS PERIOD, MY *HEART* FAR MORE OFTENER *SWELLED* WITH *THANKFULNESS* THAN *SANK* WITH *DEJECTION*.

~ CHAPTER XXXII ~

ROSAMUND HAD A *POWER* OVER *MR. RIVERS.* HER *EYE* PIERCES THE YOUNG PASTOR'S *HEART.* INDEED, HE *COULD NOT CONCEAL HIS RESPONSE.* HE *SEEMED* TO *SAY,* WITH HIS *SAD, RESOLUTE LOOK,* "I *LOVE YOU* AND I *KNOW* YOU *PREFER ME,* BUT MY *HEART* IS *ALREADY LAID* ON A *SACRED ALTAR.* IT WILL *SOON* BE *NO MORE* THAN A *SACRIFICE CONSUMED.*"

I AM *COME* TO *SEE* HOW YOU ARE *SPENDING* YOUR *HOLIDAY.*

I HAVE *BROUGHT* YOU A *BOOK* FOR *EVENING SOLACE.*

IS THIS *PORTRAIT* LIKE?

LIKE *WHOM?* I DID NOT *OBSERVE* IT *CLOSELY.*

YOU *DID,* MR. RIVERS. WHO IS IT *LIKE?*

MISS *OLIVER,* I PRESUME.

TO *REWARD* YOU FOR THE *ACCURATE* GUESS, I WILL *PROMISE* TO *PAINT YOU* A *DUPLICATE.*

WOULD IT *COMFORT,* OR WOULD IT *WOUND YOU* TO *HAVE* IT?

THAT I SHOULD *LIKE* TO *HAVE* IT IS *CERTAIN:* WHETHER IT WOULD BE *JUDICIOUS* OR WISE IS *ANOTHER QUESTION.*

SHE *LIKES YOU,* I AM *SURE.*

DOES SHE LIKE *ME?*

CERTAINLY; BETTER THAN SHE LIKES *ANYONE* ELSE.

SHE **TALKS** OF YOU **CONTINUALLY**: THERE IS **NO SUBJECT** SHE **ENJOYS** SO MUCH OR **TOUCHES** UPON SO **OFTEN**.

IT IS **VERY PLEASANT** TO **HEAR** THIS. **VERY**: GO ON FOR ANOTHER **QUARTER** OF AN **HOUR**.

BUT **WHERE** IS THE **USE** OF **GOING ON**, WHEN YOU ARE **PROBABLY** FORGING A **FRESH CHAIN** TO **FETTER** YOUR **HEART**?

DON'T **IMAGINE** SUCH **HARD THINGS**. SHE IS **TALKING** TO ME WITH HER **SWEE VOICE**, **SMILING** AT ME WITH THESE **CORAL LIPS**. SHE IS **MINE** - I AM **HERS**

HUSH! SAY **NOTHING** - MY **HEART** IS FULL OF **DELIGHT** - MY **SENSES** ARE **ENTRANCED** - LET THE **TIME** I **MARKED** PASS IN **PEACE**.

NOW. THAT **LITTLE SPACE** WAS GIVEN TO **DELIRIUM** AND **DELUSION**. I **RESTED** MY **TEMPLES** ON THE **BREAST** OF **TEMPTATION**.

HER **PROMISES** ARE **HOLLOW** - HER **OFFERS FALSE**.

IT IS **STRANGE** THAT WHILE I **LOVE** ROSAMUND OLIVER SO **WILDLY**, I **KNOW** THAT SHE WOULD **NOT** MAKE ME A **GOOD WIFE**; SHE IS **NOT** THE **PARTNER SUITED** TO ME.

TWELVE MONTHS' **RAPTURE** WOULD SUCCEED A **LIFETIME** OF **REGRET**.

STRANGE, INDEED!

SHE **IS LOVELY**. SHE IS **WELL NAMED** THE **ROSE OF THE WORLD**, INDEED!

AND **MAY** I NOT **PAINT** ONE **LIKE** IT FOR **YOU**?

CUI BONO?

NO.

WHAT IS THE **MATTER**?

NOTHING IN THE WORLD. **GOOD-AFTERNOON**.

WELL! THAT **CAPS** THE **GLOBE**!

I SAW HIM **TEAR** A **NARROW SLIP** FROM THE **MARGIN**; AND, WITH ONE **HASTY NOD**, HE **VANISHED**.

WHEN MR. ST. JOHN **WENT**, IT WAS **BEGINNING TO SNOW**; THE WHIRLING **STORM** CONTINUED **ALL NIGHT**. THE NEXT DAY, A **KEEN WIND** BROUGHT **FRESH** AND **BLINDING FALLS**; BY **TWILIGHT** THE **VALLEY** WAS ALMOST **IMPASSABLE**. I HEARD A **NOISE**: THE **WIND**, I THOUGHT, SHOOK THE **DOOR**. NO; IT WAS **ST. JOHN RIVERS**.

ANY **ILL NEWS?** HAS ANYTHING **HAPPENED?** WHY ARE YOU **COME?**

RATHER AN **INHOSPITABLE QUESTION**: BUT SINCE YOU **ASK** IT, I **ANSWER** SIMPLY TO HAVE A **LITTLE TALK** WITH YOU.

~ CHAPTER ~
~ XXXIII ~

I GOT **TIRED** OF MY **MUTE BOOKS** AND **EMPTY ROOMS**. BESIDES, SINCE **YESTERDAY** I HAVE EXPERIENCED THE **EXCITEMENT** OF A **PERSON** TO WHOM A **TALE** HAS BEEN **HALF-TOLD**, AND WHO IS **IMPATIENT** TO HEAR THE **SEQUEL**.

I **BEGAN** TO FEAR HIS **WITS** WERE **TOUCHED**. HE **SAT** FOR HALF AN HOUR, SAYING LITTLE: HIS EYE DWELLING **DREAMILY** ON THE **GLOWING GRATE**. THEN...

IT IS **FAIR** TO **WARN YOU** THAT THIS **STORY** WILL SOUND SOMEWHAT **HACKNEYED** IN YOUR **EARS**. **STALE DETAILS** OFTEN **REGAIN** A DEGREE OF **FRESHNESS** WHEN THEY **PASS** THROUGH **NEW LIPS**.

TWENTY YEARS AGO, A **POOR CURATE** - NEVER **MIND** HIS **NAME** AT THE MOMENT - FELL IN **LOVE** WITH A **RICH MAN'S DAUGHTER**. SHE **MARRIED HIM** AGAINST THE **ADVICE** OF HER **FRIENDS**, WHO CONSEQUENTLY **DISOWNED** HER IMMEDIATELY AFTER THE **WEDDING**.

BEFORE **TWO YEARS** PASSED, THE **RASH PAIR** WERE BOTH **DEAD**. I HAVE **SEEN** THEIR **GRAVE**.

THEY LEFT A **DAUGHTER**. **CHARITY** CARRIED THE **FRIENDLESS THING** TO THE **HOUSE** OF ITS **RICH MATERNAL RELATIONS**; IT WAS **REARED** BY AN **AUNT**-IN-LAW CALLED - I COME TO **NAMES** NOW -

MRS. REED OF **GATESHEAD**.

=GASP!=

YOU **START**. DID YOU HEAR A **NOISE?**

HE **WENT** ON WITH THE **REST** OF MY **OWN HISTORY**.

...SHE **LEFT LOWOOD SCHOOL** TO BE A **GOVERNESS**. THERE, AGAIN, YOUR **FATES** ARE **ANALOGOUS**. SHE **UNDERTOOK** THE **EDUCATION** OF THE **WARD** OF A CERTAIN **MR. ROCHESTER** --

MR. RIVERS!

-- I CAN **GUESS** YOUR **FEELINGS**, BUT **RESTRAIN** THEM FOR A WHILE.

I HEARD THE **STORY** OF MY **WEDDING-DAY**.

...THIS YOUNG GIRL HAD **LEFT** THORNFIELD HALL IN THE **NIGHT**. EVERY **RESEARCH** AFTER HER **COURSE** HAD BEEN IN **VAIN**.

YET THAT SHE SHOULD BE **FOUND** IS BECOME A **MATTER** OF **SERIOUS** URGENCY.

ADVERTISEMENTS HAVE BEEN PUT IN **ALL** THE PAPERS.

I **RECEIVED** THESE DETAILS IN A **LETTER** FROM A **SOLICITOR** CALLED **MR. BRIGGS**.

HE TALKS OF A **JANE EYRE**: I KNEW A **JANE ELLIOTT**.

YESTERDAY, MY **SUSPICIONS** WERE AT **ONCE** RESOLVED INTO **CERTAINTY**.

MY **SIGNATURE** FROM THE **PORTRAIT**.

MR. BRIGGS SOUGHT **AFTER** YOU TO **TELL** YOU THAT YOUR **UNCLE**, MR. EYRE OF MADEIRA, IS **DEAD**; THAT HE HAS **LEFT** YOU **ALL** HIS **PROPERTY**, AND THAT **YOU** ARE NOW **RICH** —

— MERELY THAT — **NOTHING** MORE.

I! – **RICH?** HOW **MUCH** AM I **WORTH?**

TWENTY THOUSAND POUNDS.

WELL – IF YOU HAD COMMITTED A **MURDER**, AND I HAD **TOLD YOU** YOUR **CRIME** WAS **DISCOVERED**, YOU COULD **SCARCELY** LOOK MORE **AGHAST**.

IT **PUZZLES** ME TO **KNOW** WHY MR. **BRIGGS WROTE** TO YOU ABOUT **ME**.

OH, THE CLERGY ARE **OFTEN** APPEALED TO ABOUT **ODD** MATTERS.

NO; THAT DOES NOT **SATISFY** ME! I **MUST** KNOW **MORE** ABOUT IT.

YOU ARE **NOT**, PERHAPS, **AWARE** THAT I AM YOUR **NAMESAKE?** – THAT I WAS **CHRISTENED** ST. JOHN **EYRE** RIVERS?

NO, INDEED! I **REMEMBER** NOW SEEING YOUR **INITIAL 'E'** WRITTEN IN **BOOKS** YOU HAVE LENT ME.

MY **MOTHER'S** NAME WAS **EYRE**. SHE HAD **TWO BROTHERS**; ONE A **CLERGYMAN**, WHO MARRIED **MISS JANE REED**, OF **GATESHEAD** --

-- THE OTHER, JOHN EYRE, ESQ., MERCHANT, LATE OF FUNCHAL, MADEIRA.

UNCLE JOHN LEFT HIS PROPERTY TO HIS BROTHER THE CLERGYMAN'S ORPHAN DAUGHTER, OVERLOOKING US IN CONSEQUENCE OF A QUARREL, NEVER FORGIVEN.

YOUR MOTHER WAS MY FATHER'S SISTER? MY UNCLE JOHN WAS YOUR UNCLE JOHN?

YOU, DIANA AND MARY, THEN, ARE MY COUSINS.

WE ARE COUSINS; YES.

THIS WAS WEALTH INDEED! WEALTH TO THE HEART! THIS WAS A BLESSING AND EXHILARATING; NOT LIKE THE PONDEROUS GIFT OF GOLD.

OH, I AM GLAD! - I AM GLAD!

YOU WERE SERIOUS WHEN I TOLD YOU YOU HAD GOT A FORTUNE; AND NOW, FOR A MATTER OF NO MOMENT, YOU ARE EXCITED.

WHAT CAN YOU MEAN? IT MAY BE OF NO MOMENT TO YOU; YOU HAVE SISTERS; BUT I HAD NOBODY; AND NOW THREE RELATIONS ARE BORN INTO MY WORLD FULL-GROWN. I SAY AGAIN, I AM GLAD!

THOSE WHO HAD SAVED MY LIFE, I COULD NOW BENEFIT. THEY WERE UNDER A YOKE - I COULD FREE THEM:

THE INDEPENDENCE, THE AFFLUENCE WHICH WAS MINE, MIGHT BE THEIRS TOO. WERE WE NOT FOUR? FIVE THOUSAND POUNDS EACH.

WRITE TO DIANA AND MARY AND TELL THEM TO COME HOME DIRECTLY FOR THE FORTUNE THAT HAS ACCRUED TO THEM.

TO YOU, YOU MEAN.

JANE, I WILL BE YOUR BROTHER - MY SISTERS WILL BE YOUR SISTERS - WITHOUT THIS SACRIFICE OF YOUR JUST RIGHTS.

I, WEALTHY - GORGED WITH GOLD I NEVER EARNED AND DO NOT MERIT!

YOU, PENNILESS?!

AND THE SCHOOL, MISS EYRE? IT MUST NOW BE SHUT UP, I SUPPOSE?

NO, I WILL RETAIN MY POST OF MISTRESS TILL YOU FIND A SUBSTITUTE.

I WAS ABSOLUTELY RESOLVED. THE INSTRUMENTS OF TRANSFER WERE DRAWN OUT: ST. JOHN, DIANA, MARY, AND I, EACH BECAME POSSESSED OF A COMPETENCY.

~ CHAPTER ~
~ XXXIV ~

IT WAS **NEAR CHRISTMAS** BY THE TIME **ALL** WAS SETTLED. I NOW **CLOSED** MORTON SCHOOL. HANNAH, ST. JOHN'S **SERVANT**, **HELPED** ME TO PUT **EVERYTHING** IN ORDER AT **MOOR HOUSE** READY FOR DIANA AND MARY'S **ARRIVAL**.

I **TRUST** WHEN THIS IS **OVER**, YOU WILL **LOOK** A LITTLE **HIGHER** THAN **DOMESTIC ENDEARMENTS** AND **HOUSEHOLD JOYS**.

THE **BEST THINGS** THE WORLD HAS!

NO, JANE, NO: **THIS** WORLD IS NOT THE SCENE OF **FRUITION**; DO NOT **ATTEMPT** TO **MAKE** IT SO.

ST. JOHN, I **THINK** YOU ARE ALMOST **WICKED** TO TALK SO. I AM **DISPOSED** TO BE AS **CONTENT** AS A **QUEEN**, AND YOU TRY TO **STIR** ME UP TO **RESTLESSNESS**! TO WHAT END?

TO THE **END** OF TURNING TO **PROFIT** THE **TALENTS** WHICH **GOD** HAS COMMITTED TO YOUR **KEEPING**.

DON'T CLING SO **TENACIOUSLY** TO **TIES** OF THE **FLESH**.

EVERYTHING WAS **ARRANGED** WITH **MATHEMATICAL PRECISION.** ENOUGH **COAL** AND **PEAT** WERE STOCKED TO KEEP UP **GOOD FIRES** IN **EVERY ROOM.** THE **LAST** TWO DAYS, HANNAH AND I BAKED **CHRISTMAS CAKES** AND **MINCE PIES.** WHEN ALL WAS **FINISHED**, I THOUGHT **MOOR HOUSE** AS **COMPLETE** A **MODEL** OF **BRIGHT MODEST SNUGNESS** WITHIN, AS IT WAS A **SPECIMEN** OF **WINTRY WASTE** WITHOUT.

THE **EVENTFUL THURSDAY** AT LENGTH **CAME.** THEY WERE **EXPECTED** ABOUT **DARK.** ST. JOHN ARRIVED FIRST.

ARE YOU **AT LAST** SATISFIED WITH **HOUSEMAID'S WORK**?

PLEASE **ACCOMPANY** ME ON A **GENERAL INSPECTION.**

NOT A **SYLLABLE** DID HE **UTTER** INDICATING **PLEASURE** IN THE **IMPROVED** ASPECT OF HIS **ABODE.**

THE **SILENCE** DAMPED ME. I COMPREHENDED ALL AT **ONCE** THAT IT WOULD BE A **TRYING THING** TO BE HIS **WIFE.**

ST. JOHN, ARE YOUR **PLANS** YET **UNCHANGED?**

UNCHANGED AND **UNCHANGEABLE.** MY **DEPARTURE** FROM **ENGLAND** IS NOW **FIXED** FOR THE ENSUING YEAR.

AND **ROSAMUND OLIVER?**

ROSAMUND IS ABOUT TO BE **MARRIED** TO **MR. GRANBY:** A **WELL-CONNECTED** AND MOST **ESTIMABLE PERSONAGE,** AND **GRANDSON** AND **HEIR** TO **SIR FREDERIC GRANBY.**

THE **MATCH** MUST HAVE BEEN **GOT UP HASTILY.** THEY **CANNOT** HAVE **KNOWN** EACH OTHER **LONG.**

BUT **TWO MONTHS.** THEY **MET** IN **OCTOBER** AT THE **COUNTY BALL.** BUT WHERE THERE ARE **NO OBSTACLES** TO A UNION, WHERE THE CONNECTION IS IN **EVERY** POINT **DESIRABLE,** DELAYS ARE **UNNECESSARY.**

JANE, WHAT ARE **YOU** DOING?

LEARNING **GERMAN.**

I WANT YOU TO **GIVE UP GERMAN** AND LEARN **HINDOSTANEE.** IT IS THE **LANGUAGE** I AM **STUDYING.** WOULD YOU **HELP** ME UNTIL I **DEPART** IN **THREE MONTHS'** TIME?

IF YOU ARE IN **EARNEST.**

IN SUCH **EARNEST** THAT I **MUST** HAVE IT SO.

I HAD **NOT FORGOTTEN** MR. ROCHESTER. **NOT** FOR A **MOMENT.** I **WROTE** TO **MRS. FAIRFAX** AND WAS **ASTONISHED** WHEN A **FORTNIGHT PASSED** WITHOUT A **REPLY.** WHEN **TWO MONTHS** WORE AWAY, I WROTE **AGAIN.**

WHEN **HALF A YEAR** WASTED IN **VAIN EXPECTANCY,** MY **HOPE** DIED OUT, AND THEN I FELT **DARK INDEED.**

BY DEGREES, ST. JOHN ACQUIRED A CERTAIN **INFLUENCE** OVER ME THAT **TOOK AWAY** MY **LIBERTY** OF **MIND.** I **DAILY WISHED** MORE TO **PLEASE HIM;** BUT TO DO SO, I FELT THAT I MUST **DISOWN** HALF MY **NATURE.**

JANE, COME **WITH** ME TO **INDIA.**

GOD AND **NATURE** INTENDED YOU FOR A **MISSIONARY'S WIFE.** YOU ARE **FORMED** FOR **LABOUR,** NOT FOR **LOVE.**

A **MISSIONARY'S WIFE** YOU **MUST - SHALL** BE.

YOU SHALL BE MINE: I CLAIM YOU - NOT FOR MY PLEASURE, BUT FOR MY SOVEREIGN'S SERVICE.

ALAS! IF I JOIN ST. JOHN, I ABANDON HALF MYSELF.

I WANT A WIFE: THE SOLE HELPMEET I CAN INFLUENCE EFFICIENTLY IN LIFE, AND RETAIN ABSOLUTELY TILL DEATH.

I AM READY TO GO TO INDIA, IF I MAY GO FREE.

YOUR ANSWER REQUIRES A COMMENTARY. IT IS NOT CLEAR.

SEEK A WIFE ELSEWHERE THAN IN ME.

I WILL GIVE THE MISSIONARY MY ENERGIES, BUT NOT MYSELF.

DO YOU THINK GOD WILL BE SATISFIED WITH HALF AN OBLIGATION? I CANNOT ACCEPT ON HIS BEHALF A DIVIDED ALLEGIANCE.

IT MUST BE ENTIRE.

OH! I WILL GIVE MY HEART TO GOD.

YOU DO NOT WANT IT.

WE MUST BE MARRIED; AND UNDOUBTEDLY ENOUGH OF LOVE WOULD FOLLOW UPON MARRIAGE TO RENDER THE UNION RIGHT EVEN IN YOUR EYES.

I SCORN YOUR IDEA OF LOVE AND THE COUNTERFEIT SENTIMENT YOU OFFER:

YES, ST. JOHN, AND I SCORN YOU WHEN YOU OFFER IT.

I SCARCELY EXPECTED TO HEAR THAT EXPRESSION FROM YOU.

I HAVE DONE AND UTTERED NOTHING TO DESERVE SCORN.

FORGIVE ME THE WORDS; BUT YOU INTRODUCED A TOPIC WE SHOULD NEVER DISCUSS. ABANDON YOUR SCHEME OF MARRIAGE.

IT IS A LONG-CHERISHED SCHEME; BUT I SHALL URGE YOU NO FURTHER AT PRESENT.

DO NOT FORGET THAT IF YOU REJECT IT, IT IS NOT ME YOU DENY, BUT GOD.

~ CHAPTER ~
~ XXXV ~

ST. JOHN MADE ME FEEL WHAT SEVERE PUNISHMENT A GOOD YET STERN MAN CAN INFLICT ON ONE WHO HAS OFFENDED HIM. WITHOUT ONE OVERT ACT OF HOSTILITY, HE CONTRIVED TO IMPRESS ME MOMENTLY WITH THE CONVICTION THAT I WAS PUT BEYOND THE PALE OF HIS FAVOUR. I FELT HOW, IF I WERE HIS WIFE, THIS GOOD MAN COULD SOON KILL ME, WITHOUT DRAWING FROM MY VEINS A SINGLE DROP OF BLOOD.

MUST WE PART IN THIS WAY, ST. JOHN? WHEN YOU GO TO INDIA, WILL YOU LEAVE ME SO, WITHOUT A KINDER WORD THAN YOU HAVE YET SPOKEN?

WHAT! DO YOU NOT GO TO INDIA?

YOU SAID I COULD NOT UNLESS I MARRIED YOU.

AND YOU WILL NOT MARRY ME! YOU ADHERE TO THAT RESOLUTION?

WHAT TERROR THOSE COLD PEOPLE CAN PUT INTO THE ICE OF THEIR QUESTIONS. HOW MUCH OF THE FALL OF THE AVALANCHE IS IN THEIR ANGER?

NO, ST. JOHN, I WILL NOT MARRY YOU.

THERE IS A POINT ON WHICH I HAVE LONG ENDURED PAINFUL DOUBT, AND I CAN GO NOWHERE TILL BY SOME MEANS THAT DOUBT IS REMOVED.

ARE YOU GOING TO SEEK MR. ROCHESTER?

I MUST FIND OUT WHAT IS BECOME OF HIM.

IT REMAINS FOR ME, THEN, TO REMEMBER YOU IN MY PRAYERS.

ST. JOHN WAS TO GO TO CAMBRIDGE. I TENDERED MY HAND, AND WISHED HIM A PLEASANT JOURNEY.

I STOOD MOTIONLESS UNDER MY HIEROPHANT'S TOUCH. MY REFUSALS WERE FORGOTTEN.

THE IMPOSSIBLE - MY MARRIAGE WITH ST JOHN - WAS FAST BECOMING THE POSSIBLE.

ALL WAS CHANGING UTTERLY WITH A SUDDEN SWEEP.

RELIGION CALLED - GOD COMMANDED.

THE DIM ROOM WAS FULL OF VISIONS.

COULD YOU DECIDE NOW?

WERE I BUT CONVINCED THAT IT IS GOD'S WILL I SHOULD MARRY YOU, I COULD VOW TO MARRY YOU HERE AND NOW!

MY PRAYERS ARE HEARD!

MY HEART BEAT FAST AND THICK. SUDDENLY IT STOOD STILL TO AN INEXPRESSIBLE FEELING THAT THRILLED IT THROUGH; AND PASSED AT ONCE TO MY HEAD AND EXTREMITIES. THE FEELING FORCED MY SENSES TO WAKE FROM THEIR TORPOR.

I HEARD A VOICE SOMEWHERE CRY.

JANE! JANE! JANE!

O GOD! WHAT IS IT?

IT WAS THE VOICE OF A HUMAN BEING - A KNOWN, LOVED, WELL-REMEMBERED VOICE - THAT OF EDWARD FAIRFAX ROCHESTER; AND IT SPOKE IN PAIN AND WOE, WILDLY, EERILY, URGENTLY.

WHAT HAVE YOU HEARD? WHAT DO YOU SEE?

I AM COMING!

WAIT FOR ME!

OH, I WILL COME!

WHERE ARE YOU?

DOWN SUPERSTITION! THIS IS NOT THY DECEPTION, NOR THY WITCHCRAFT: IT IS THE WORK OF NATURE.

SHE WAS ROUSED, AND DID - NO MIRACLE - BUT HER BEST.

THE HILLS BEYOND MARSH GLEN SENT THE ANSWER FAINTLY BACK; "WHERE ARE YOU?" I LISTENED. THE WIND SIGHED LOW IN THE FIRS: ALL WAS MOORLAND LONELINESS AND MIDNIGHT HUSH.

~ CHAPTER ~
~ XXXVI ~

THE DAYLIGHT CAME. I ROSE AT DAWN. ST. JOHN PASSED A NOTE UNDER MY DOOR...

Jane

'YOU LEFT ME TOO SUDDENLY LAST NIGHT. HAD YOU BUT STAYED A LITTLE LONGER, YOU WOULD HAVE LAID YOUR HAND ON THE CHRISTIAN'S CROSS AND THE ANGEL'S CROWN. I SHALL EXPECT YOUR DECISION WHEN I RETURN FROM CAMBRIDGE.'

'MEANTIME, WATCH AND PRAY THAT YOU ENTER NOT INTO TEMPTATION:

THE SPIRIT, I TRUST, IS WILLING, BUT THE FLESH, I SEE, IS WEAK. I SHALL PRAY FOR YOU HOURLY.

- YOURS,
  ST. JOHN.'

MY SPIRIT IS WILLING TO DO WHAT IS RIGHT; WHEN ONCE THAT WILL IS DISTINCTLY KNOWN TO ME.

ERE MANY DAYS, I WILL KNOW SOMETHING OF HIM WHOSE VOICE SEEMED LAST NIGHT TO SUMMON ME. LETTERS HAVE PROVED OF NO AVAIL - PERSONAL INQUIRY SHALL REPLACE THEM.

I AM GOING ON A JOURNEY AND SHALL BE ABSENT AT LEAST FOUR DAYS.

ALONE, JANE?

YES; IT IS TO SEE OR HEAR NEWS OF A FRIEND ABOUT WHOM I HAVE FOR SOME TIME BEEN UNEASY.

WITH HER *TRUE NATURAL DELICACY*, SHE *ABSTAINED* FROM *COMMENT*, EXCEPT THAT SHE *ASKED* ME IF I WAS *SURE* I WAS *WELL ENOUGH* TO TRAVEL. I LOOKED VERY *PALE*, SHE *OBSERVED*. I REPLIED THAT *NOTHING* AILED ME SAVE *ANXIETY OF MIND*, WHICH I HOPED SOON TO *ALLEVIATE*.

IT WAS *EASY* TO MAKE MY *FURTHER* ARRANGEMENTS; FOR I WAS *TROUBLED* WITH NO *INQUIRIES* - NO *SURMISES*.

IT WAS A *JOURNEY* OF *SIX-AND-THIRTY HOURS*.

I GAVE A *BOX* I HAD INTO THE *OSTLER'S CHARGE*, TO BE *KEPT* UNTIL I *CALLED* FOR IT...

'THE ROCHESTER ARMS'! I AM ALREADY ON MY MASTER'S VERY LANDS.

ROCHESTER ARMS

...AND HASTENED ACROSS THE *FINAL TWO MILES* TO *THORNFIELD HALL*.

HOW I LOOKED FORWARD TO CATCH THE *FIRST VIEW* OF THE WELL-KNOWN *WOODS!* AT LAST, ITS *ROOKERY* CLUSTERED *DARK*. A *LOUD CAWING* OF *CROWS* BROKE THE *MORNING STILLNESS*.

WHO WOULD BE HURT BY MY ONCE MORE TASTING THE LIFE HIS GLANCE CAN GIVE ME?

I RAVE: PERHAPS HE IS WATCHING THE SUN RISE OVER THE PYRENEES.

I LOOKED WITH *TIMOROUS JOY* TOWARDS A *STATELY HOUSE*...

...I SAW A *BLACKENED RUIN*.

I RETURNED TO THE INN.

YOU **KNOW** THORNFIELD HALL, OF **COURSE**?

YES, MA'AM, I *LIVED* THERE ONCE.

I WAS THE *LATE* MR. ROCHESTER'S *BUTLER*.

=GASP!=

THE *LATE!* IS HE *DEAD*?

I MEAN THE *PRESENT* GENTLEMAN MR. *EDWARD'S* FATHER.

GLADDENING WORDS! MY MR. ROCHESTER WAS AT *LEAST* ALIVE.

I SUPPOSE YOU ARE A STRANGER IN THESE PARTS, OR YOU WOULD HAVE HEARD WHAT *HAPPENED* LAST AUTUMN.

THORNFIELD HALL WAS *BURNT DOWN* JUST ABOUT *HARVEST* TIME. THE *FIRE* BROKE OUT AT *DEAD OF NIGHT*.

AT *DEAD* OF **NIGHT!** WAS IT **KNOWN** HOW IT **ORIGINATED?**

THEY *GUESSED*, MA'AM.

YOU ARE NOT PERHAPS *AWARE* -- THERE WAS A *LADY* -- A *LUNATIC*, KEPT IN THE *HOUSE*?

I HAVE HEARD **SOMETHING** OF IT.

THIS *LADY* TURNED OUT TO BE MR. ROCHESTER'S *WIFE!* THERE WAS A *YOUNG LADY*, A *GOVERNESS* AT THE HALL THAT MR. ROCHESTER *FELL IN LOVE* WITH. *WELL*, HE WOULD MARRY HER.

HIS *LUNATIC* WIFE WAS TAKEN *CARE* OF BY A WOMAN CALLED *MRS. POOLE*.

MRS. POOLE HAD A COMMON *FAULT*: SHE NOW AND THEN TOOK A DROP OF *GIN* OVERMUCH.

WHEN SHE WAS *FAST ASLEEP*, THE *MAD LADY* WOULD *TAKE* HER *KEYS* AND GO *ROAMING* ABOUT THE HOUSE, DOING *MISCHIEF*.

SHE *SET FIRE* TO THE *HANGINGS* OF THE *ROOM* NEXT TO HER OWN, AND *THEN* SHE MADE HER WAY TO THE *CHAMBER* THAT *HAD* BEEN THE *GOVERNESS'S*.

SHE WAS *LIKE* AS IF SHE *KNEW* SOMEHOW HOW MATTERS HAD *GONE ON*, AND HAD A *SPITE* AT HER;

BUT THERE WAS *NOBODY* SLEEPING IN IT, FORTUNATELY.

THE GOVERNESS HAD *RUN AWAY* TWO MONTHS *BEFORE*.

FOR ALL MR. ROCHESTER *SOUGHT* HER AS IF SHE HAD BEEN THE MOST *PRECIOUS* THING HE HAD IN THE *WORLD*, HE NEVER COULD HEAR A *WORD* OF HER; AND HE GREW *QUITE SAVAGE* IN HIS *DISAPPOINTMENT*:

HE NEVER *WAS* A *MILD* MAN, BUT HE GOT *DANGEROUS* AFTER HE *LOST* HER. HE WOULD BE *ALONE*, TOO.

HE SENT *MRS. FAIRFAX* THE HOUSEKEEPER AWAY TO HER FRIENDS; MISS *ADÈLE*, A WARD HE HAD, WAS PUT TO *SCHOOL*.

HE *BROKE OFF* ACQUAINTANCE WITH ALL THE *GENTRY*, AND *SHUT HIMSELF UP* LIKE A *HERMIT* AT THE HALL.

HE WOULD NOT *CROSS THE DOOR-STONES* OF THE *HOUSE*, EXCEPT AT *NIGHT*, WHEN HE WALKED LIKE A *GHOST* ABOUT THE GROUNDS AND IN THE ORCHARD AS IF HE HAD *LOST HIS SENSES*.

113

WERE *ANY OTHER* LIVES LOST?

NO — PERHAPS IT WOULD HAVE BEEN *BETTER* IF THERE *HAD.*

WHAT DO YOU *MEAN?*

POOR MR. EDWARD!

SOME SAY IT WAS A *JUST JUDGMENT* ON HIM FOR WANTING TO TAKE *ANOTHER WIFE* WHILE HE HAD ONE *LIVING:* BUT I *PITY* HIM, FOR MY PART.

YOU *SAID* HE WAS *ALIVE?*

YES: HE *IS* ALIVE; BUT *MANY* THINK HE HAD BETTER BE *DEAD.*

WHY? HOW? IS HE IN ENGLAND?

AY — AY — HE CAN'T GET OUT OF ENGLAND, I FANCY — — HE'S A *FIXTURE* NOW.

HE IS *STONE-BLIND*, IS MR. EDWARD.

I HAD DREADED *WORSE.* I HAD *DREADED* HE WAS *MAD.*

IT WAS *ALL* HIS OWN *COURAGE*, AND A BODY MAY SAY, HIS *KINDNESS* IN A WAY, MA'AM. HE *WOULDN'T LEAVE* THE HOUSE TILL *EVERYONE* ELSE WAS *OUT* BEFORE HIM.

AS HE CAME DOWN THE *GREAT STAIRCASE* AT LAST, AFTER MRS. ROCHESTER HAD *FLUNG* HERSELF FROM THE *BATTLEMENTS*, THERE WAS A *GREAT CRASH* — ALL FELL.

HE WAS *TAKEN OUT* FROM *UNDER* THE RUINS, ALIVE, BUT SADLY HURT.

ONE EYE WAS *KNOCKED OUT*, AND ONE HAND SO *CRUSHED* THAT MR. CARTER, THE SURGEON, HAD TO *AMPUTATE* IT DIRECTLY. THE *OTHER EYE* INFLAMED: HE LOST THE *SIGHT* OF THAT ALSO.

HE IS NOW *HELPLESS*, INDEED – BLIND, AND A *CRIPPLE*.

WHERE DOES HE LIVE *NOW?*

AT *FERNDEAN*, A MANOR HOUSE ON A *FARM* HE HAS, ABOUT THIRTY MILES OFF: QUITE A *DESOLATE* SPOT.

IF YOUR *POST-BOY* CAN *DRIVE ME THERE* BEFORE *DARK* THIS *DAY*, I'LL *PAY* BOTH *YOU* AND HIM *TWICE* THE HIRE YOU *USUALLY* DEMAND.

~ CHAPTER ~
~ XXXVII~

MR. ROCHESTER OFTEN SPOKE OF FERNDEAN, AND SOMETIMES WENT THERE. HIS FATHER HAD PURCHASED THE ESTATE FOR THE SAKE OF THE GAME COVERS, BUT COULD FIND NO TENANT, IN CONSEQUENCE OF ITS INELIGIBLE AND INSALUBRIOUS SITE.

FERNDEAN THEN REMAINED UNINHABITED AND UNFURNISHED, WITH THE EXCEPTION OF SOME TWO OR THREE ROOMS FOR THE ACCOMMODATION OF THE SQUIRE WHEN HE WENT THERE IN THE SEASON TO SHOOT.

DUSK AS IT WAS, I RECOGNISED HIM.

I STAYED MY STEP, ALMOST MY BREATH, AND STOOD TO WATCH HIM - ALAS! TO HIM INVISIBLE. IT WAS A SUDDEN MEETING, AND ONE IN WHICH RAPTURE WAS KEPT WELL IN CHECK BY PAIN. I HAD NO DIFFICULTY IN RESTRAINING MY VOICE FROM EXCLAMATION, MY STEP FROM HASTY ADVANCE.

IN HIS COUNTENANCE, I SAW A CHANGE: THAT LOOKED DESPERATE AND BROODING - THAT REMINDED ME OF SOME WRONGED AND FETTERED WILD BEAST OR BIRD, DANGEROUS TO APPROACH IN HIS SULLEN WOE.

THE CAGED EAGLE, WHOSE GOLD-RINGED EYES CRUELTY HAS EXTINGUISHED, MIGHT LOOK AS LOOKED THAT SIGHTLESS SAMSON.

WILL YOU TAKE MY ARM, SIR? THERE IS A HEAVY SHOWER COMING ON. HAD YOU NOT BETTER GO IN?

LEAVE ME ALONE.

MR. ROCHESTER GROPED HIS WAY BACK TO THE HOUSE AND CLOSED THE DOOR. I NOW DREW NEAR AND KNOCKED.

RINGGGG!

WHEN YOU GO IN, TELL YOUR MASTER THAT A PERSON WISHES TO SPEAK TO HIM, BUT DO NOT GIVE MY NAME.

I DON'T THINK HE WILL SEE YOU. HE REFUSES EVERYBODY.

MARY - HOW ARE YOU?

IS IT REALLY YOU, MISS, COME AT THIS LATE HOUR TO THIS LONELY PLACE?

MOMENTS LATER...

YOU ARE TO SEND IN YOUR NAME AND YOUR BUSINESS.

IS THAT WHAT HE RANG FOR?

YES.

GIVE THE TRAY TO ME; I WILL CARRY IT IN.

Lie down!

YELP!

GIVE ME THE WATER, MARY.

WHAT IS THE **MATTER?**

DOWN, PILOT!

THIS IS **YOU, MARY,** IS IT **NOT?**

MARY IS IN THE **KITCHEN.**

WHO IS **THIS?**

WHO IS THIS?

ANSWER ME - SPEAK AGAIN!

WILL YOU HAVE A LITTLE MORE **WATER,** SIR? I **SPILT** HALF OF WHAT WAS IN THE **GLASS.**

WHO IS IT? **WHAT** IS IT? WHO **SPEAKS?**

PILOT KNOWS ME, AND **JOHN** AND **MARY** KNOW I AM **HERE.** I **CAME** ONLY THIS **EVENING.**

GREAT **GOD!** WHAT **DELUSION** HAS **COME OVER** ME? WHAT **SWEET MADNESS** HAS **SEIZED** ME?

NO DELUSION - NO **MADNESS:**

YOUR **MIND,** SIR, IS TOO **STRONG** FOR **DELUSION,** YOUR **HEALTH** TOO **SOUND** FOR FRENZY.

WHERE IS THE **SPEAKER?** IS IT ONLY A **VOICE?**

OH! I CANNOT **SEE,** OR I MUST **FEEL,** OR MY **HEART** WILL **STOP** AND MY **BRAIN** BURST.

WHATEVER, WHOEVER YOU ARE, BE **PERCEPTIBLE** TO THE **TOUCH,** OR I **CANNOT LIVE!**

HER **VERY FINGERS!** HER **SMALL, SLIGHT FINGERS!** IF **SO,** THERE **MUST** BE **MORE** OF HER.

IS IT *JANE*? THIS IS HER *SHAPE* - THIS IS HER *SIZE* --

AND *THIS* HER VOICE. SHE IS *ALL HERE*: HER *HEART*, TOO. *GOD BLESS YOU*, SIR! I AM *GLAD* TO BE SO *NEAR YOU* AGAIN.

JANE EYRE! *JANE EYRE*!

MY *DEAR MASTER*, I AM *JANE EYRE*:

I HAVE *FOUND* YOU *OUT* - I AM *COME BACK* TO YOU.

BUT I *CANNOT* BE SO *BLEST*, AFTER *ALL* MY *MISERY*.

IT IS A *DREAM*; SUCH *DREAMS* AS I HAVE *HAD* AT NIGHT WHEN I HAVE *CLASPED* HER ONCE *MORE* TO MY *HEART*, AS I *DO* NOW; AND *KISSED* HER - AND FEEL THAT SHE *LOVED* ME, AND *TRUSTED* THAT SHE WOULD NOT LEAVE ME.

WHICH I *NEVER WILL*, SIR, FROM THIS *DAY*.

NEVER WILL, SAYS THE *VISION*? BUT I ALWAYS *WOKE* AND FOUND IT AN *EMPTY MOCKERY*.

AND YOU *DO NOT* LIE DEAD IN SOME *DITCH*, UNDER SOME *STREAM*?

AND YOU ARE *NOT A PINING OUTCAST* AMONGST *STRANGERS*?

NO, SIR! I AM AN *INDEPENDENT WOMAN* NOW.

INDEPENDENT! WHAT *DO* YOU *MEAN*, JANE?

MY *UNCLE* IN *MADEIRA* IS *DEAD*, AND HE *LEFT* ME *FIVE THOUSAND POUNDS*.

AH! THIS IS *PRACTICAL* - THIS IS *REAL*! I SHOULD *NEVER* DREAM *THAT*.

BESIDES, THERE IS THAT *PECULIAR VOICE* OF HERS, SO *ANIMATING* AND *PIQUANT*, AS WELL AS *SOFT*:

IT *CHEERS* MY *WITHERED HEART*; IT PUTS *LIFE* INTO IT.

WHAT! ARE YOU AN *INDEPENDENT WOMAN*?

A *RICH WOMAN*?

QUITE RICH, SIR. I AM MY **OWN** MISTRESS.

AND YOU WILL **STAY** WITH ME?

CERTAINLY - UNLESS YOU **OBJECT**.

I WILL BE YOUR **NEIGHBOUR**, YOUR **NURSE**, YOUR **HOUSEKEEPER**, YOUR **COMPANION** - TO **READ** TO YOU, TO **WALK** WITH YOU, TO **WAIT** ON YOU, TO BE **EYES** AND **HANDS** TO YOU.

YOU SHALL **NOT** BE LEFT **DESOLATE**, SO **LONG** AS I **LIVE**.

YOU --

-- HAVE AN **AFFECTIONATE** **HEART** AND A **GENEROUS** **SPIRIT**, WHICH **PROMPT** YOU TO MAKE **SACRIFICES** FOR THOSE YOU **PITY**.

I **SUPPOSE** I SHOULD **NOW** ENTERTAIN **NONE** BUT **FATHERLY** FEELINGS FOR YOU:

DO YOU **THINK** SO? COME, TELL ME.

I WILL **THINK** WHAT YOU **LIKE**, SIR.

I AM **CONTENT** TO BE ONLY YOUR **NURSE**, IF YOU THINK IT **BETTER**.

BUT YOU **CANNOT** ALWAYS BE MY NURSE, *JANET: YOU ARE **YOUNG** - YOU **MUST** MARRY **ONE** DAY.

I DON'T **CARE** ABOUT BEING **MARRIED**.

YOU **SHOULD** **CARE**, JANET: IF I **WERE** WHAT I **ONCE** WAS, I WOULD **TRY** TO MAKE YOU CARE - BUT - A **SIGHTLESS** **BLOCK**!

HE **RELAPSED** AGAIN INTO GLOOM.

I RESUMED A **LIVELIER** VEIN OF CONVERSATION.

IT IS **TIME** SOMEONE UNDERTOOK TO **REHUMANISE** YOU, FOR I SEE YOU ARE BEING **METAMORPHOSED** INTO A **LION**.

YOUR **HAIR** REMINDS ME OF **EAGLES'** FEATHERS; WHETHER YOUR **NAILS** ARE GROWN LIKE **BIRDS'** CLAWS OR NOT, I HAVE **NOT** YET **NOTICED**.

ON THIS **ARM**, I HAVE NEITHER **HAND** NOR **NAILS**. IT IS A **MERE** **STUMP** - A **GHASTLY** **SIGHT**!

DON'T YOU **THINK**, JANE?

IT IS A **PITY** TO **SEE** IT; AND A **PITY** TO SEE YOUR **EYES** - AND THE **SCAR** OF FIRE ON YOUR **FOREHEAD** --

121

Mr. Rochester would sometimes call her Janet.

-- AND THE **WORST** OF IT IS, ONE IS IN **DANGER** OF **LOVING** YOU **TOO WELL** FOR ALL THIS, AND MAKING **TOO MUCH** OF YOU.

I **THOUGHT** YOU WOULD BE **REVOLTED**, JANE, WHEN YOU SAW MY **ARM**, AND MY **CICATRISED** VISAGE.

DID YOU? DON'T **TELL ME** SO - LEST I SHOULD **SAY** SOMETHING **DISPARAGING** ABOUT YOUR **JUDGMENT**.

NOW LET ME **LEAVE YOU** IN AN **INSTANT** TO MAKE A **BETTER FIRE**.

CAN YOU **TELL** WHEN THERE IS A **GOOD FIRE?**

YES; WITH THE **RIGHT EYE** I SEE A **GLOW** - A **RUDDY HAZE**.

AND YOU **SEE** THE **CANDLES?**

VERY **DIMLY** - EACH IS A **LUMINOUS CLOUD**.

CAN YOU **SEE ME?**

NO, MY **FAIRY:** BUT I AM **ONLY** TOO **THANKFUL** TO **HEAR** AND **FEEL YOU**.

WHEN DO YOU TAKE **SUPPER?**

I **NEVER** TAKE **SUPPER**.

BUT YOU **SHALL** HAVE SOME **TO-NIGHT**. I AM **HUNGRY**: SO ARE **YOU**, I **DARESAY**, ONLY YOU **FORGET**.

SUMMONING **MARY**, I SOON HAD THE **ROOM** IN MORE **CHEERFUL** ORDER: I **PREPARED** HIM, LIKEWISE, A **COMFORTABLE** REPAST. MY **SPIRITS** WERE **EXCITED**, AND WITH **PLEASURE** AND **EASE** I **TALKED** TO HIM DURING **SUPPER**, AND FOR A **LONG TIME AFTER**. WITH **HIM** I WAS AT **PERFECT EASE**, BECAUSE I **KNEW** I **SUITED** HIM; ALL I SAID OR **DID** SEEMED EITHER TO **CONSOLE** OR **REVIVE** HIM. IN HIS **PRESENCE** I **THOROUGHLY** LIVED; AND HE **LIVED** IN **MINE**.

IF A **MOMENT'S SILENCE** BROKE THE CONVERSATION, HE WOULD TURN **RESTLESS**, TOUCH ME, THEN SAY, "JANE".

122

YOU ARE **ALTOGETHER** A **HUMAN BEING**, JANE? YOU ARE **CERTAIN** OF THAT?

I **CONSCIENTIOUSLY** BELIEVE SO, MR. **ROCHESTER.**

HOW CAN IT **BE** THAT **JANE** IS WITH ME, AND SAYS SHE **LOVES** ME? WILL SHE NOT **DEPART** AS **SUDDENLY** AS SHE **CAME?**

TO-MORROW, I FEAR, I SHALL **FIND** HER NO **MORE.**

YOUR **EYEBROWS** ARE **SCORCHED.**

I WILL **APPLY** SOMETHING THAT WILL MAKE THEM **GROW** AS **BROAD** AND **BLACK** AS **EVER.**

WHERE IS THE **USE** OF DOING ME **GOOD** IN ANY WAY, BENEFICENT **SPIRIT,** **WHEN**, AT SOME **FATAL MOMENT,** YOU WILL AGAIN **DESERT** ME --

-- FOR **ME** REMAINING AFTERWARDS **UNDISCOVERABLE?**

HAVE YOU A **POCKET-COMB** ABOUT YOU, SIR, TO **COMB** OUT THIS **SHAGGY, BLACK MANE?**

I FIND YOU RATHER **ALARMING,** WHEN I **EXAMINE** YOU CLOSE AT **HAND.**

AM I **HIDEOUS,** JANE?

VERY, SIR; YOU ALWAYS **WERE,** YOU KNOW.

HUMPH! THE **WICKEDNESS** HAS NOT BEEN TAKEN OUT OF YOU, **WHEREVER** YOU HAVE SOJOURNED.

YET I HAVE **BEEN** WITH **GOOD PEOPLE -- FAR** BETTER THAN **YOU.**

WHO THE **DEUCE** HAVE YOU **BEEN** WITH?

YOU SHALL **NOT** GET IT OUT OF ME **TO-NIGHT,** SIR; YOU MUST **WAIT** TILL **TO-MORROW.**

TO LEAVE MY TALE **HALF** TOLD **WILL,** YOU KNOW, BE A SORT OF **SECURITY** THAT I SHALL **APPEAR** AT YOUR **BREAKFAST-TABLE** TO **FINISH** IT.

YOU *MOCKING CHANGELING* - *FAIRY-BORN* AND *HUMAN-BRED!*

YOU MAKE ME *FEEL* AS I HAVE *NOT FELT* THESE *TWELVE MONTHS.*

NOW I'LL LEAVE YOU: I HAVE BEEN TRAVELLING THESE *LAST THREE DAYS,* AND I *BELIEVE* I AM *TIRED.*

JUST *ONE WORD,* JANE: WERE THERE ONLY *LADIES* IN THE HOUSE WHERE YOU HAVE BEEN?

HA-HA-HA!

A *GOOD IDEA!*

I *SEE* I HAVE THE *MEANS* OF *FRETTING* HIM OUT OF HIS *MELANCHOLY* FOR *SOME TIME* TO *COME.*

VERY *EARLY* THE NEXT *MORNING,* I HEARD HIM *UP* AND *ASTIR,* WANDERING FROM *ONE ROOM* TO *ANOTHER.*

GOOD MORNING, SIR.

IS *MISS EYRE* HERE?

WHICH *ROOM* DID YOU PUT HER INTO?

WAS IT *DRY?* IS SHE *UP?*

GO AND *ASK* HER IF SHE *WANTS* ANYTHING; AND *WHEN* SHE WILL *COME DOWN.*

IT IS A *BRIGHT, SUNNY* MORNING, SIR.

THE *RAIN* IS *OVER* AND *GONE,* AND THERE IS A *TENDER SHINING* AFTER IT; *YOU* SHALL HAVE A *WALK* SOON.

OH, YOU ARE *INDEED* THERE, MY *SKYLARK!*

I *HEARD* ONE OF YOUR KIND AN *HOUR AGO,* SINGING *HIGH* OVER THE *WOOD:* BUT ITS SONG HAD NO *MUSIC* FOR ME, ANY MORE THAN THE *RISING SUN* HAD RAYS.

ALL THE *MELODY* ON *EARTH* IS CONCENTRATED IN MY *JANE'S* TONGUE TO *MY* EAR - I AM *GLAD* IT IS NOT *NATURALLY* A *SILENT* ONE.

ALL THE *SUNSHINE* I CAN *FEEL* IS IN HER *PRESENCE.*

THE *WATER* STOOD IN MY *EYES* TO HEAR THIS *AVOWAL* OF HIS *DEPENDENCE;* JUST AS IF A *ROYAL EAGLE,* CHAINED TO A *PERCH,* MUST *ENTREAT* A *SPARROW* TO BECOME ITS *PURVEYOR.*

124

MOST OF THE MORNING WAS SPENT IN THE **OPEN AIR.**

CRUEL, CRUEL **DESERTER!**
OH **JANE,** WHAT DID I FEEL WHEN I DISCOVERED YOU HAD **FLED** FROM **THORNFIELD,** AND WHEN I COULD **NOWHERE FIND YOU:** AND, AFTER **EXAMINING** YOUR **APARTMENT,** ASCERTAINED THAT YOU HAD TAKEN **NO MONEY,** NOR **ANYTHING** WHICH COULD SERVE AS AN **EQUIVALENT!**

WHAT COULD MY **DARLING DO,** I ASKED, LEFT **DESTITUTE** AND **PENNILESS?**

AND **WHAT DID** SHE DO? LET ME **HEAR NOW.**

THUS URGED, I BEGAN THE **NARRATIVE OF MY EXPERIENCE** FOR THE **LAST YEAR.** I **SOFTENED CONSIDERABLY** WHAT RELATED TO THE **THREE DAYS** OF **WANDERING** AND **STARVATION,** BECAUSE TO HAVE TOLD HIM **ALL** WOULD HAVE BEEN TO INFLICT **UNNECESSARY PAIN.**

I WOULD **NEVER** HAVE **FORCED YOU** TO BE MY **MISTRESS.**

I **LOVE** YOU **FAR TOO WELL** AND **TOO TENDERLY** TO BE YOUR **TYRANT.**

I WOULD HAVE **GIVEN** YOU **HALF MY FORTUNE,** WITHOUT DEMANDING SO MUCH AS A **KISS** IN **RETURN,** RATHER THAN HAVE YOU **FLING** YOURSELF **FRIENDLESS** ON THE **WIDE WORLD.**

YOU HAVE **ENDURED,** I AM **CERTAIN, MORE** THAN YOU HAVE **CONFESSED** TO ME.

WELL, **WHATEVER** MY **SUFFERINGS** HAD BEEN, THEY WERE **VERY SHORT.**

I THEN PROCEEDED TO **TELL** HIM HOW I HAD BEEN RECEIVED AT **MOOR HOUSE;** HOW I HAD OBTAINED THE OFFICE OF **SCHOOL-MISTRESS,** ETC.

OF COURSE, **ST. JOHN RIVERS'** NAME CAME IN **FREQUENTLY** IN THE **PROGRESS** OF MY **TALE.**

THIS **ST. JOHN,** THEN, IS YOUR **COUSIN?**

YES.

YOU HAVE **SPOKEN** OF HIM **OFTEN:** DO YOU **LIKE** HIM?

HE WAS A VERY **GOOD** MAN, SIR; I COULD NOT **HELP** LIKING HIM.

A **GOOD MAN.** DOES THAT MEAN A **RESPECTABLE, WELL-CONDUCTED** MAN OF **FIFTY?** OR **WHAT** DOES IT MEAN?

ST. JOHN WAS ONLY **TWENTY-NINE,** SIR.

JEUNE ENCORE. IS HE OF **LOW STATURE, PHLEGMATIC,** AND **PLAIN?**

IS HIS **BRAIN SOFT?** HE **MEANS** WELL: BUT YOU **SHRUG** YOUR **SHOULDERS** TO HEAR HIM **TALK?**

HE TALKS LITTLE, SIR - BUT HIS BRAIN IS FIRST-RATE.

AN EDUCATED MAN --

-- HIS APPEARANCE - A SORT OF RAW CURATE, HALF STRANGLED WITH HIS WHITE NECKCLOTH, AND STILTED UP ON HIS THICK-SOLED HIGH-LOWS, EH?

HE IS A HANDSOME MAN: WELL-DRESSED, TALL, FAIR, WITH BLUE EYES, AND A GRECIAN PROFILE.

DAMN HIM!

PERHAPS YOU WOULD RATHER NOT SIT ANY LONGER ON MY KNEE, MISS EYRE?

WHY NOT, MR. ROCHESTER?

THE PICTURE YOU HAVE JUST DRAWN IS SUGGESTIVE OF A RATHER TOO OVERWHELMING CONTRAST.

YOUR WORDS HAVE DELINEATED VERY PRETTILY A GRACEFUL APOLLO --

-- YOUR EYES DWELL ON A VULCAN - A REAL BLACKSMITH, BROWN, BROAD-SHOULDERED; AND BLIND AND LAME INTO THE BARGAIN.

I NEVER THOUGHT OF IT BEFORE; BUT YOU CERTAINLY ARE RATHER LIKE VULCAN, SIR.

WELL, YOU CAN LEAVE ME, MA'AM: BUT BEFORE YOU GO, YOU WILL BE PLEASED TO ANSWER ME A QUESTION OR TWO.

WHAT QUESTIONS, MR. ROCHESTER?

THEN FOLLOWED A CROSS-EXAMINATION!

ST. JOHN MADE YOU SCHOOL-MISTRESS OF MORTON **BEFORE** HE KNEW YOU WERE HIS **COUSIN?**

YES.

YOU WOULD **OFTEN** SEE HIM AT **YOUR COTTAGE** NEAR THE **SCHOOL?**

NOW AND THEN. HE **STUDIED** A GOOD DEAL.

DID HE TEACH **YOU** ANYTHING?

A LITTLE **HINDOSTANEE.**

OF WHAT **USE** COULD HINDOSTANEE BE TO **YOU?**

HE **INTENDED** ME TO **GO** WITH HIM TO INDIA.

AH! **HERE** I REACH THE **ROOT** OF THE MATTER. HE **WANTED** YOU TO **MARRY HIM?**

HE **ASKED** ME TO MARRY HIM.

THAT IS A **FICTION** - AN IMPUDENT INVENTION TO VEX ME.

I BEG YOUR **PARDON,** IT IS THE **LITERAL TRUTH:**

HE **ASKED** ME **MORE** THAN **ONCE,** AND WAS AS **STIFF** ABOUT **URGING** HIS **POINT** AS **EVER YOU** COULD BE.

MISS EYRE, I **REPEAT** IT, YOU **CAN LEAVE ME.** **WHY** DO YOU REMAIN PERTINACIOUSLY **PERCHED** ON MY **KNEE,** WHEN I HAVE **GIVEN** YOU **NOTICE** TO **QUIT?**

BECAUSE I AM **COMFORTABLE** THERE.

NO, JANE, YOU ARE **NOT** COMFORTABLE THERE, BECAUSE YOUR **HEART** IS **NOT** WITH **ME:**

IT IS WITH THIS **COUSIN** - THIS **ST. JOHN.**

OH, TILL THIS **MOMENT,** I THOUGHT MY LITTLE JANE WAS ALL MINE!

SHAKE ME **OFF,** THEN, SIR, FOR I'LL **NOT** LEAVE YOU OF MY **OWN ACCORD.**

HE IS **NOT** MY **HUSBAND,** NOR **EVER** WILL BE.

HE **DOES NOT LOVE ME:** I DO NOT **LOVE HIM.**

HE **LOVES** - AS HE **CAN** LOVE, AND **THAT** IS **NOT** AS **YOU** LOVE - A **BEAUTIFUL YOUNG LADY** CALLED **ROSAMUND.**

HE WANTED TO MARRY ME **ONLY** BECAUSE HE THOUGHT I SHOULD MAKE A SUITABLE **MISSIONARY'S WIFE,** WHICH **SHE** WOULD **NOT** HAVE DONE.

HITHERTO, I HAVE **HATED** TO BE **HELPED** - TO BE **LED**. BUT IT IS **PLEASANT** TO FEEL MY **HAND** CIRCLED BY JANE'S LITTLE **FINGERS**.

JANE **SUITS** ME: DO I SUIT **HER**?

TO THE **FINEST FIBRE** OF MY **NATURE**, SIR.

THE CASE BEING **SO**, WE HAVE **NOTHING** IN THE **WORLD** TO WAIT FOR: WE MUST BE **MARRIED** INSTANTLY.

JANE! YOU **THINK** ME, I **DARESAY**, AN **IRRELIGIOUS DOG**: BUT MY **HEART** SWELLS WITH **GRATITUDE** TO THE **BENEFICENT GOD** OF THIS **EARTH** JUST NOW.

OF **LATE** - ONLY OF LATE - I BEGAN TO SEE THE **HAND OF GOD** IN MY **DOOM**. I BEGAN TO EXPERIENCE **REMORSE, REPENTANCE**; I BEGAN **SOMETIMES** TO **PRAY**.

LAST **MONDAY NIGHT**, A **SINGULAR MOOD** CAME OVER ME: ONE IN WHICH **GRIEF** REPLACED **FRENZY**. I HAD **LONG** HAD THE **IMPRESSION** THAT SINCE I COULD **NOWHERE FIND** YOU, YOU **MUST BE DEAD**.

LATE THAT **NIGHT**, I **SUPPLICATED GOD**; THAT, IF IT SEEMED **GOOD** TO HIM, I MIGHT **SOON** BE **TAKEN** FROM THIS **LIFE**, AND ADMITTED TO **THAT WORLD** TO **COME**, WHERE THERE WAS **STILL HOPE** OF **REJOINING JANE**.

I **LONGED** FOR THEE, **JANET**! BOTH WITH **SOUL** AND **FLESH**!

THE **ALPHA** AND **OMEGA** OF MY **HEART'S** WISHES BROKE **INVOLUNTARILY** FROM MY **LIPS** IN THE WORDS...

JANE! JANE! JANE!

DID YOU **SPEAK** THESE **WORDS** ALOUD?

I **DID**, JANE. IF ANY **LISTENER** HAD **HEARD** ME, HE WOULD HAVE THOUGHT ME **MAD**, I **PRONOUNCED** THEM WITH SUCH **FRANTIC** ENERGY.

AND IT WAS **LAST MONDAY NIGHT**, SOMEWHERE NEAR **MIDNIGHT**?

YES; BUT THE **TIME** IS OF **NO CONSEQUENCE**: WHAT **FOLLOWED** IS THE **STRANGE POINT**.

YOU WILL **THINK** ME **SUPERSTITIOUS.** A **VOICE** - I CANNOT **TELL** WHENCE THE VOICE **CAME,** BUT I **KNOW** WHOSE **VOICE** IT **WAS** - REPLIED...

I AM COMING: WAIT FOR ME...

WHERE ARE YOU?

AND A **MOMENT AFTER,** WENT **WHISPERING** ON THE **WIND** THE WORDS...

COOLER AND **FRESHER** AT THE **MOMENT** THE **GALE** SEEMED TO **VISIT** MY **BROW:** I COULD HAVE **DEEMED** THAT IN SOME **WILD, LONE** SCENE, I AND **JANE** WERE **MEETING.**

IN **SPIRIT,** I BELIEVE WE **MUST** HAVE MET. **YOU** NO DOUBT **WERE,** AT THAT **HOUR,** IN **UNCONSCIOUS SLEEP,** JANE:

PERHAPS YOUR **SOUL WANDERED** FROM ITS **CELL** TO **COMFORT** MINE; FOR THOSE WERE **YOUR** ACCENTS, AS **CERTAIN** AS I **LIVE,** THEY WERE **YOURS!**

IT WAS ON **MONDAY NIGHT** - NEAR **MIDNIGHT** - THAT I **TOO** HAD RECEIVED THE **MYSTERIOUS** SUMMONS: **THOSE** WERE THE **VERY** WORDS BY WHICH I **REPLIED** TO IT.

I MADE **NO DISCLOSURE** IN **RETURN;** MY TALE WOULD MAKE A **PROFOUND** IMPRESSION ON THE **MIND** OF MY **HEARER:** AND THAT MIND, YET FROM ITS **SUFFERINGS** TOO PRONE TO **GLOOM,** NEEDED **NOT** THE **DEEPER SHADE** OF THE **SUPERNATURAL.**

YOU **CANNOT** NOW **WONDER** THAT WHEN YOU **ROSE** UPON ME SO **UNEXPECTEDLY** LAST NIGHT, I HAD DIFFICULTY IN **BELIEVING** YOU ANY **OTHER** THAN A **MERE VOICE** AND **VISION,**

SOMETHING THAT WOULD **MELT** TO **SILENCE** AND **ANNIHILATION,** AS THE **MIDNIGHT** WHISPER AND **MOUNTAIN** ECHO HAD MELTED **BEFORE.**

NOW, I THANK **GOD**! I **KNOW** IT TO BE OTHERWISE. YES, I THANK **GOD**!

I THANK MY **MAKER**, THAT, IN THE **MIDST** OF **JUDGMENT**, HE HAS **REMEMBERED MERCY**.

I HUMBLY **ENTREAT** MY **REDEEMER** TO GIVE ME **STRENGTH** TO LEAD HENCEFORTH A **PURER** LIFE THAN I HAVE DONE **HITHERTO**!

THEN HE STRETCHED HIS **HAND** OUT TO BE **LED**.

I **TOOK** THAT **DEAR** HAND, HELD IT A MOMENT TO MY **LIPS**, THEN LET IT PASS ROUND MY **SHOULDER**: BEING SO MUCH **LOWER** OF **STATURE** THAN HE, I SERVED BOTH FOR HIS **PROP** AND GUIDE. WE ENTERED THE **WOOD**, AND WENDED **HOMEWARD**.

~ CHAPTER ~
~ XXXVIII ~
CONCLUSION

I **MARRIED** HIM. A **QUIET** WEDDING, WE HAD: HE AND I, THE **PARSON** AND **CLERK**, WERE **ALONE** PRESENT. I WROTE TO MOOR HOUSE AND TO **CAMBRIDGE** IMMEDIATELY; TO SAY WHAT I HAD **DONE**: FULLY EXPLAINING ALSO **WHY** I HAD THUS ACTED.

DIANA AND **MARY** APPROVED THE STEP **UNRESERVEDLY**.

DIANA SAYS THAT SHE WILL **JUST** GIVE ME **TIME** TO GET OVER THE **HONEYMOON**, AND THEN SHE WILL **COME** AND **SEE** ME!

SHE HAD **BETTER NOT** WAIT TILL **THEN**, JANE. IF SHE **DOES**, SHE WILL BE **TOO LATE**, FOR OUR **HONEYMOON** WILL **SHINE** OUR **LIFE** LONG:

ITS **BEAMS** WILL ONLY **FADE** OVER **YOUR** GRAVE OR MINE.

HOW **ST. JOHN** RECEIVED THE NEWS, I **DON'T** KNOW: HE NEVER ANSWERED THE **LETTER** IN WHICH I **COMMUNICATED** IT.

YET SIX MONTHS **AFTER** HE **WROTE** TO ME; **WITHOUT**, HOWEVER, MENTIONING MR. **ROCHESTER'S NAME** OR ALLUDING TO MY **MARRIAGE**. HIS **LETTER** WAS THEN **CALM**, AND, THOUGH VERY **SERIOUS**, KIND.

HE HAS MAINTAINED A **REGULAR**, THOUGH NOT **FREQUENT**, CORRESPONDENCE EVER **SINCE**.

I HAVE **NOW** BEEN MARRIED **TEN YEARS.** I **KNOW** WHAT IT IS TO LIVE ENTIRELY **FOR** AND WITH WHAT I **LOVE** BEST ON EARTH. I **HOLD** MYSELF **SUPREMELY BLEST** - **BLEST** BEYOND WHAT **LANGUAGE** CAN **EXPRESS;** BECAUSE I AM MY HUSBAND'S LIFE AS **FULLY** AS HE IS **MINE.**

MR. **ROCHESTER** CONTINUED **BLIND** THE **FIRST** TWO YEARS OF OUR **UNION.** ONE **MORNING...**

JANE, HAVE YOU A **GLITTERING ORNAMENT** ROUND YOUR NECK? AND HAVE YOU A **PALE BLUE DRESS** ON?

YES!

FOR **SOME TIME,** I HAVE **FANCIED** THAT THE **OBSCURITY** CLOUDING **ONE EYE** WAS BECOMING **LESS DENSE;** NOW I AM **SURE** OF IT.

HE AND I WENT UP TO **LONDON.** HE HAD THE **ADVICE** OF AN **EMINENT OCULIST;** AND HE **EVENTUALLY RECOVERED** THE **SIGHT** OF THAT **ONE EYE.**

HE HAS **MY EYES** AS THEY **ONCE** WERE.

YES - SO **LARGE, BLACK** AND **BRILLIANT.**

I **THANK GOD,** WHO HAS **AGAIN** TEMPERED **JUDGMENT** WITH **MERCY.**

DIANA AND **MARY RIVERS** ARE BOTH **MARRIED:** ALTERNATELY, ONCE EVERY **YEAR, THEY** COME TO SEE **US,** AND **WE** GO TO SEE **THEM.** DIANA'S HUSBAND IS A **CAPTAIN** IN THE **NAVY;** MARY'S IS A **CLERGYMAN.**

ST. JOHN RIVERS WENT TO **INDIA.** HE ENTERED ON THE **PATH** HE **MARKED** FOR HIMSELF. HE IS **UNMARRIED:** HE **NEVER WILL** MARRY NOW. HIS GLORIOUS **SUN** HASTENS TO ITS **SETTING.** I KNOW THAT A **STRANGER'S** HAND WILL WRITE TO ME NEXT, TO SAY THAT THE **GOOD** AND **FAITHFUL SERVANT** HAS BEEN CALLED AT **LENGTH** INTO THE **JOY** OF HIS **LORD.**

AND WHY **WEEP** FOR **THIS?** NO **FEAR** OF **DEATH** WILL DARKEN ST. JOHN'S LAST **HOUR**

HIS **MIND** WILL BE **UNCLOUDED,** HIS **HEART** WILL BE **UNDAUNTED,** HIS **HOPE** WILL BE **SURE,** AND HIS **FAITH STEADFAST.**

Jane Eyre

The End

Charlotte Brontë

(1816 –1855)

"Literature cannot be the business of a woman's life..."

Poet Laureate Robert Southeys' letter to Charlotte Brontë in 1837

George Richmond, chalk, 1850 National Portrait Gallery, London

Charlotte Brontë was born on 21st April 1816, at 74 Market Street in the village of Thornton near Bradford, Yorkshire. She was one of six children born to Maria Branwell and Patrick Brontë: Maria (1814), Elizabeth (1815), Charlotte (1816), Patrick Branwell (who was known as Branwell, 1817), Emily (1818) and Anne (1820).

Her father, Patrick, was an Irish Anglican clergyman and writer, born in County Down, Ireland, in 1777. His surname was originally Brunty, but he decided to change his name, probably to give the impression of a more well-to-do background, giving the world the now familiar "Brontë." Charlotte's mother, Maria, was born in 1785, to a prosperous merchant family in Cornwall. Patrick and Maria met in Hartshead, Yorkshire, while she was helping her aunt with the domestic side of running a school.

In April 1820, when Charlotte was four years old, the family moved a short distance from Thornton to Haworth, where Patrick had been appointed perpetual curate of the church. Maria's sister, Elizabeth joined them a year later to help look after the children and to care for her sister, who was suffering from the final stages of cancer. She died in September 1821 - Charlotte was still only five years old.

The Parsonage at Haworth was a literary household. From early childhood, the Brontë children had written about the lives, wars and sufferings of people who lived in their own imaginary kingdoms. The story goes that Branwell had been given a set of toy soldiers in June 1826, and from these the children developed imaginary worlds of their own. Charlotte and Branwell wrote stories about their country — **"Angria"** — and Emily and Anne wrote articles and poems about theirs — **"Gondal"**. These sagas, plays, poems and stories were written down in handmade "little books" — books that they made from paper sheets stitched together. In a letter to author and biographer Elizabeth Gaskell, Patrick Brontë wrote:

"When mere children, as soon as they could read and write, Charlotte and her brother and sisters used to invent and act little plays of their own."

In July 1824 Maria (ten) and Elizabeth (nine) were sent to the Clergy Daughter's School at Cowan Bridge, near Kirkby Lonsdale in Lancashire. Charlotte (eight) and Emily (six) joined them there in August. Life at boarding school must have been grim. Maria became ill and was sent home in February 1825; she died at Haworth in May. Elizabeth fell ill that same month and, like her sister, was sent home; she died just a few months later. Both sisters died of tuberculosis (also known as "consumption") and as a result of their deaths, Emily and Charlotte were withdrawn from the school. These events obviously had a great impact on Charlotte, who drew on the experience for *Jane Eyre* when she described Lowood School and the death of Helen Burns.

In fact much of the novel mirrors Charlotte's own life. Charlotte, like Jane, spent many years as a governess for a number of families - a career which she viewed with some distaste (a view which appears in Chapter 30 of this book, at the bottom of page 95). Having no personal fortune and few respectable ways of earning a living, this was the only socially acceptable option for many genteel young ladies. Emily and Anne also became governesses, although Emily's career as a teacher was short-lived; it is reported that she told her pupils at Miss Patchett's School in Halifax that she much preferred the school dog to any of them!

In 1842, Charlotte and Emily travelled to Brussels to study at the Pensionnat Heger — a boarding school run by Constantin Heger and his wife. Their Aunt Elizabeth Branwell paid for this trip, with the plan that they would set up their own school at the Parsonage when they returned. However, the girls were forced to return to England later that year when their Aunt Elizabeth died — just as in this book when Jane Eyre returns to Gateshead Hall when her Aunt Reed is on her death-bed.

Charlotte travelled alone to Brussels in January 1843 to take up a teaching post at Pensionnat Heger. This second stay was not a happy one: she was lonely without her sister, homesick, and had become deeply attached to Constantin Heger. She returned to Haworth a year later in January 1844. Her time at Pensionnat Heger became the inspiration for parts of two other books: *The Professor* and *Villette;* and her attraction to the married Constantin would seem to reflect Jane Eyre's love for Mr. Rochester.

Of the three sisters, Anne was the most successful teacher; but by 1845 the entire family, including Branwell, were all back at The Parsonage. Branwell returned home somewhat in disgrace for "proceedings bad beyond expression" - most likely a love affair with his employer's wife.

After Charlotte's return home, the sisters finally started on their project to start a school of their own. This turned out to be a total failure — they didn't manage to attract a single student! However that was probably to the world's advantage. Over the years, the sisters had continued their writing, and in 1846 — having abandoned the idea of starting a school - they decided to publish a selection of their poems. The title was simply *Poems* and it was published under different author names: Currer (Charlotte), Ellis (Emily) and Acton (Anne) Bell. One thousand copies of the book were printed, at a cost of around £50, which they funded themselves. The book received some favourable reviews, but sold only two copies in the first year.

Charlotte gave an explanation for these psuedonyms:

> "Averse to personal publicity, we veiled our own names under those of Currer, Ellis and Acton Bell; the ambiguous choice being dictated by a sort of conscientious scruple at assuming Christian names positively masculine, while we did not like to declare ourselves women, because - without at that time suspecting that our mode of writing and thinking was not what is called 'feminine' - we had a vague impression that authoresses are liable to be looked on with prejudice; we had noticed how critics sometimes use for their chastisement the weapon of personality, and for their reward, a flattery, which is not true praise."

In the same year that *Poems* was published, Charlotte also completed her first novel, *The Professor*. It was rejected by a number of publishers, but despite that, Charlotte remained undeterred. The following year saw the publication of Charlotte's *Jane Eyre*, Emily's *Wuthering Heights*, and Anne's *Agnes Grey;* all published under their assumed "Bell" names.

The sisters hid behind their assumed names until 1848, when Anne's second novel, *The Tenant of Wildfell Hall* was published; and the sisters were forced to reveal their true identities.

These first successes for the sisters were overshadowed by sadness. Their brother, Branwell, had been subjecting himself to alcohol and opium abuse for many years; and he died in 1848 – officially from tuberculosis, but thought to be brought on by his drug and drink habits. He was just thirty-one years old.

At the same time, Anne and Emily both became ill with tuberculosis. Emily died in December 1848, aged thirty.

Charlotte took Anne (who was now her only sibling) to Scarborough in May 1849, hoping that the sea air would help to cure her. Unfortunately, Anne died just four days after their arrival, aged only twenty-nine. She was buried in Scarborough so that their father didn't have to suffer the pain of yet another family funeral.

Shortly afterwards, Charlotte wrote:

"A year ago – had a prophet warned me how I should stand in June 1849 – how stripped and bereaved….I should have thought – this can never be endured…"

Charlotte turned to her writing for comfort in these bleak times; and her next novel, *Shirley* was published in October 1849. She was now quite famous and attracted a great deal of attention. For instance, during one of her many visits to London she not only met her literary idol, W.M. Thackeray, but she also had her portrait painted by popular High Society artist George Richmond (reproduced at the top of page 134).

Her next novel, *Villette* published in 1853, was to be her last.

During this time, Charlotte had also attracted the personal attention of her father's curate, the Reverend Arthur Bell Nicholls. Charlotte initially rejected Reverend Nicholls' proposal for marriage,

probably due to her father thinking that he was not worthy of his now-famous daughter. Eventually, however, he softened, and Charlotte married Reverend Nicholls in Haworth Church on 29th June 1854, and they spent their honeymoon in Ireland. Once again, this is mirrored in *Jane Eyre*, where Jane attracts the interest of a religious man, and also where Mr. Rochester suggests sending her away to Ireland. More interestingly, however, these actual events took place after *Jane Eyre* was written!

Charlotte became pregnant; and at the same time, her health began to decline. Elizabeth Gaskell, Charlotte's earliest biographer, writes that she was attacked by

"sensations of perpetual nausea and ever-recurring faintness."

Charlotte and her unborn child died on 31st March 1855, three weeks before her thirty-ninth birthday. Her death certificate gives the cause of death as phthisis (tuberculosis).

Her husband, Reverend Nicholls, looked after Charlotte's father, Patrick, for six years until his death in June 1861 at the age of eighty-four.

Other than Patrick, none of the Brontës of Haworth enjoyed a long life, and none of them had any children to carry on the literary name.

"Gentle, soft dream, nestling in my arms now,
you will fly, too, as your sisters have all fled before you:"

(from Jane Eyre, written while her younger sisters were alive).

The Brontë Family Tree

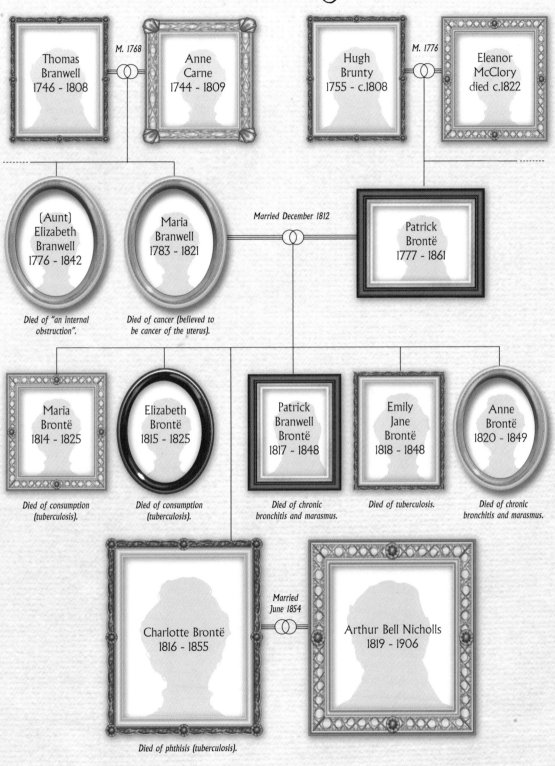

Thomas Branwell 1746 - 1808 — M. 1768 — Anne Carne 1744 - 1809

Hugh Brunty 1755 - c.1808 — M. 1776 — Eleanor McClory died c.1822

(Aunt) Elizabeth Branwell 1776 - 1842
Died of "an internal obstruction".

Maria Branwell 1783 - 1821
Died of cancer (believed to be cancer of the uterus).

Married December 1812

Patrick Brontë 1777 - 1861

Maria Brontë 1814 - 1825
Died of consumption (tuberculosis).

Elizabeth Brontë 1815 - 1825
Died of consumption (tuberculosis).

Patrick Branwell Brontë 1817 - 1848
Died of chronic bronchitis and marasmus.

Emily Jane Brontë 1818 - 1848
Died of tuberculosis.

Anne Brontë 1820 - 1849
Died of chronic bronchitis and marasmus.

Charlotte Brontë 1816 - 1855
Died of phthisis (tuberculosis).

Married June 1854

Arthur Bell Nicholls 1819 - 1906

Key:
Parent of ——————
Married ≡≡OO≡≡

Due to the lack of official records of births, deaths and marriages within this period, the above information is derived from extensive research and is as accurate as possible from the limited sources available.

A Chronology

1816	**21st April:** Charlotte is born at Thornton, Yorkshire, the third daughter of Patrick Brontë and Maria Branwell Brontë.
1817	**26th June:** Patrick Branwell Brontë is born.
1818	**30th July:** Emily Jane Brontë is born.
1820	**17th January:** Anne Brontë is born.
	February: Patrick Senior is appointed curate at Haworth.
	April: the Brontë family moves to Haworth.
1821	**September:** Maria Brontë dies of cancer. Her sister, Elizabeth Branwell, moves in with the family.
1824	**July:** Elizabeth and Maria are sent to the Clergy Daughters' School at Cowan Bridge, Lancashire.
	August: Charlotte and Emily are also sent to the Clergy Daughters' School (the school became a model for Lowood School in Jane Eyre).
1825	Elizabeth and Maria both return home from school in ill health. Maria dies in May, Elizabeth dies in June (both from tuberculosis, or "consumption"). Charlotte and Emily are removed from the school and sent home.
1826-1831	To entertain themselves, the children fill the pages of miniature homemade books with stories about imaginary kingdoms, inspired by some toy soldiers given to Branwell as a gift.
1831	**January:** Charlotte attends Miss Wooler's school at Roe Head, Mirfield. Here she meets lifelong friends Mary Taylor and Ellen Nussey.
1832	**June:** Charlotte leaves Roe Head to return home and teach her sisters.
1835	**July:** Charlotte returns to Roe Head as a teacher, taking Emily with her as a free pupil.
	October: Emily returns home, and Anne takes her place.
1838	**December:** Charlotte resigns her position and returns to Haworth.
1839	**March:** Charlotte rejects a marriage proposal from Reverend Henry Nussey, Ellen's brother.
	May to July: Charlotte works as a governess in Lothersdale.
	July: Charlotte rejects another marriage proposal, this time from Mr. Pryce — an Irish curate.
1841	Charlotte works as a governess at Rawdon from March to December.
1842	**February:** Charlotte and Emily go to Brussels to study languages at the Pensionnat Heger.
	October: Their Aunt Elizabeth dies.
	November: Charlotte and Emily return to Haworth.
1843	**January:** Charlotte returns to Brussels alone, but is lonely and becomes depressed. She forms an attachment to Constantin Heger, the head of the school, whose intellect appeals to her. Madame Heger's jealousy necessitates her departure.
1844	With all of the siblings now back at Haworth, the family try to start a school at the Haworth parsonage, but it is not a success.
1845	The Reverend Arthur Bell Nicholls becomes curate at Haworth.
1846	**April:** Charlotte, Emily, and Anne publish at their own expense a joint volume of *Poems* by Currer, Ellis, and Acton Bell. Only two copies are sold. Charlotte's novel *The Professor* is rejected by publishers.
	August: Charlotte begins *Jane Eyre* while caring for her father who was recovering from an eye operation.
1847	**October:** *Jane Eyre* is published, and is an immediate success. It starts off life as *Jane Eyre: An Autobiography Edited by Currer Bell* as if Jane Eyre was a real person and Charlotte Brontë, working under her assumed name of Currer Bell was merely the editor.
1848	**September:** Charlotte starts *Shirley*; Branwell dies of tuberculosis.
	December: Emily dies of tuberculosis. Anne also becomes ill.
1849	**May:** Charlotte tries to nurse Anne back to health and takes her to Scarborough. She dies four days after they arrive there.
	October: *Shirley – A Tale by Currer Bell* is published.
1849-1851	Charlotte travels frequently. She is invited to London as the guest of her publisher, where she meets Thackeray.
	She also visits the Lake District, Scotland, and Manchester, where she meets with Elizabeth Gaskell, her future biographer.
1851	**April:** She rejects a marriage proposal from James Taylor, a member of her publishing house.
1853	**January:** *Villette,* a novel set in Brussels is published, still by Currer Bell.
1854	**June:** Charlotte marries her fourth suitor, Arthur Bell Nichols, her father's curate. She begins but does not finish a novel, *Emma*.
1855	**March:** Charlotte dies during her pregnancy and is buried at The Parsonage at Haworth.
1857	**March:** Elizabeth Gaskell's *The Life of Charlotte Brontë* is published.
	June: Her previously rejected novel *The Professor* is published posthumously.

A Letter from Charlotte

This is a letter written by Charlotte Brontë on 24th September 1847 to her publisher, Messrs. Smith, Elder and Co., thanking them for their punctuation of her manuscript for *Jane Eyre*. Interestingly, she signs it as C. Bell, which was the name under which she wrote *Jane Eyre* (see page 135). Seeing the finished book today, it is hard to imagine a time when the classic tale didn't exist; but like any other work, it had to be conceived and written. This letter, then, is like a time capsule - linking us back to when the book was still a work-in-progress:

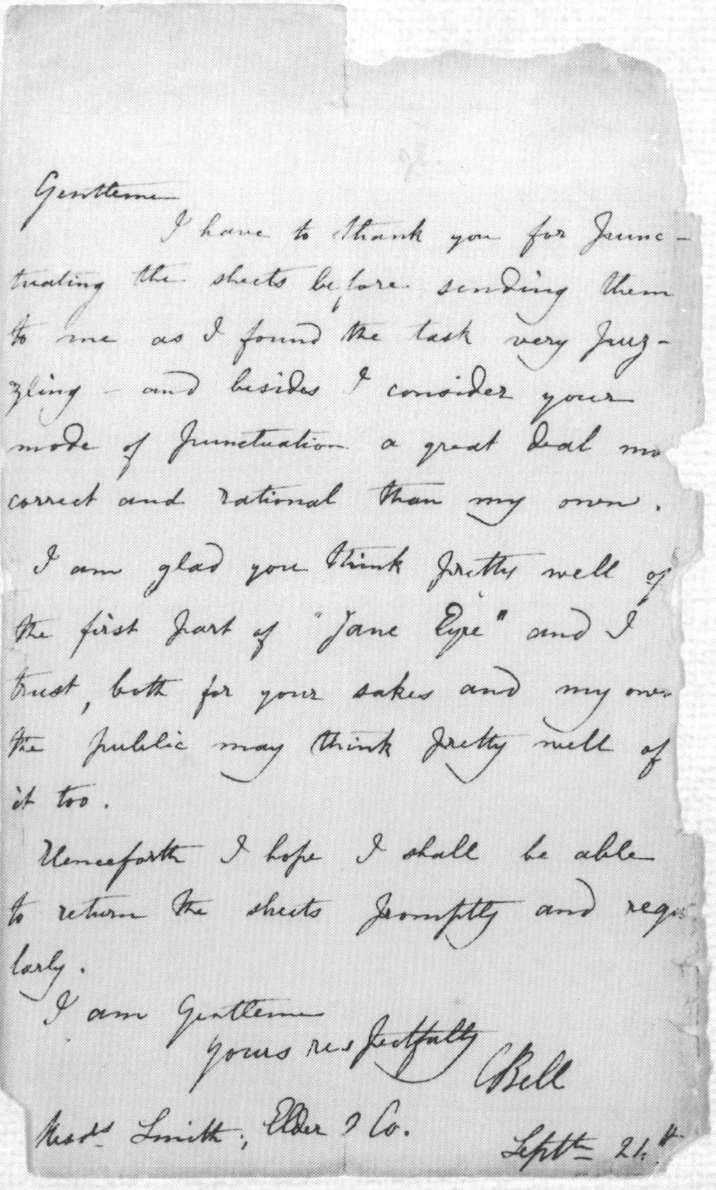

"Gentlemen,

I have to thank you for punctuating the sheets before sending them to me as I found the task very puzzling - and besides I consider your mode of punctuation a great deal mo[re] correct and rational than my own.

I am glad you think pretty well of the first part of "*Jane Eyre*" and I trust, for both your sakes and my own the public may think pretty well of it too.

Henceforth I hope that I shall be able to return the sheets promptly and regularly.

I am Gentlemen
Yours respectfully
C Bell"

To Messrs. Smith, Elder and Co.,
24th September (1847)

In order to create two versions of the same book, the story is first adapted into two scripts: Original Text and Quick Text. While the degree of complexity changes for each script, the artwork remains the same for both books.

A page from the script of *Jane Eyre* showing the two versions of text.

The pencil drawing of page 91.

The rough sketch created from the above script.

Jane Eyre artist John M. Burns guides us through the creation process:

"First off, I make A5-ish thumbnails of the page layout. These are transferred to the art board which is then masked with tape while at the same time making any alterations to the page layout.

I then start the finished pencil drawings.

The next process is to ink these drawings. For Jane Eyre I mixed the ink I used (black, yellow ochre, and burnt umber). This gives the drawings a slight period look and is not such a contrast as black.

The ink drawing in this case is more a guide for the colour. However I will work up an inked drawing if I feel a flat colour will work.

After the ink stage the fun begins (the painting)."

The inked image, ready for colouring.

Adding colour brings the page and its characters to life.

Each character has a detailed Character Study drawn. This is useful for the artist to refer to and ensures continuity throughout the book.

Jane Eyre character study

The final stage is to add the captions, sound effects, and dialogue speech bubbles from the script. These are laid on top of the coloured pages. Two versions of each page are lettered, one for each of the two versions of the book (Original Text and Quick Text).

These are then saved as final artwork pages and compiled into the finished book.

Original Text

ISBN:
978-1-906332-06-8

THE CLASSIC NOVEL
BROUGHT TO LIFE IN FULL COLOUR!

Quick Text

ISBN:
978-1-906332-08-2

THE FULL STORY IN QUICK MODERN
ENGLISH FOR A FAST-PACED READ!

LOOK OUT FOR MORE TITLES
IN THE CLASSICAL COMICS RANGE

Frankenstein:
The Graphic Novel

Published: 29th September 2008 • 144 Pages • £9.99
• Script Adaptation: Jason Cobley • Linework: Declan Shalvey
• Colours: Jason Cardy & Kat Nicholson • Art Direction: Jon Haward • Letters: Terry Wiley

True to the original novel (rather than the square-headed Boris Karloff image from the films!) Declan's naturally gothic artistic style is a perfect match for this epic tale. Frankenstein is such a well known title; yet the films strayed so far beyond the original novel that many people today don't realise how this classic horror tale deals with such timeless subjects as alienation, empathy and understanding beyond appearance. Another great story, beautifully crafted into a superb graphic novel.

ISBN: 978-1-906332-15-0

ISBN: 978-1-906332-16-7

A Christmas Carol:
The Graphic Novel

Published: 13th October 2008 • 160 Pages • £9.99
• Script Adaptation: Sean Michael Wilson • Pencils: Mike Collins
• Inks: David Roach • Colours: James Offredi • Letters: Terry Wiley

A full-colour graphic novel adaptation of the much-loved Christmas story from the great Charles Dickens. Set in Victorian England and highlighting the social injustice of the time, we see one Ebenezer Scrooge go from oppressor to benefactor when he gets a rude awakening to how his life is, and how it should be. With sumptuous artwork and wonderful characters, this magical tale is a must-have for the festive season.

ISBN: 978-1-906332-17-4

ISBN: 978-1-906332-18-1

OTHER CLASSICAL COMICS TITLES:

Great Expectations
Published: January 2009
Original Text   978-1-906332-09-9
Quick Text   978-1-906332-11-2

Romeo & Juliet
Published: July 2009
Original Text   978-1-906332-19-8
Plain Text   978-1-906332-20-4
Quick Text   978-1-906332-21-1

Richard III
Published: March 2009
Original Text   978-1-906332-22-8
Plain Text   978-1-906332-23-5
Quick Text   978-1-906332-24-2

Dracula
Published: September 2009
Original Text   978-1-906332-25-9
Quick Text   978-1-906332-26-6

The Tempest
Published: May 2009
Original Text   978-1-906332-29-7
Plain Text   978-1-906332-30-3
Quick Text   978-1-906332-31-0

The Canterville Ghost
Published: October 2009
Original Text   978-1-906332-27-3
Quick Text   978-1-906332-28-0

For more information visit www.classicalcomics.com

TEACHERS' RESOURCES

T o accompany each title in our series of graphic novels, we also publish a set of teachers' resources. These widely acclaimed photocopiable books are designed by teachers, for teachers, to help meet the requirements of the UK curriculum guidelines. Aimed at upper Key Stage 2 and above, each book provides exercises that cover structure, listening, understanding, motivation and comprehension as well as key words, themes and literary techniques. Although the majority of the tasks focus on the use of language in order to align with the revised framework for teaching English, you will also find many cross-curriculum topics, covering areas within history, ICT, drama, reading, speaking, writing and art; and with a range of skill levels, they provide many opportunities for differentiated teaching and the tailoring of lessons to meet individual needs.

Classical Comics
Study Guide: Jane Eyre
Black and white,
spiral bound A4 (making it
easy to photocopy).

Price: £19.99
ISBN: 978-1-906332-12-9

Published: October 2008

**DIFFERENTIATED
TEACHING AT
YOUR FINGERTIPS!**

"Because the exercises feature illustrations from the graphic novel, they provide an immediate link for students between the book and the exercise – however they can also be used in conjunction with any traditional text; and many of the activities can be used completely stand-alone. I think the guide is fantastic and I look forward to using it. I know it will be a great help and lead to engaging lessons . It is easy to use, another major asset. Seriously: well done, well done, well done!"

Kornel Kossuth,
Head of English, Head of General Studies

"Thank you! These will be fantastic for all our students. It is a brilliant resource and to have the lesson ideas too are great. Thanks again to all your team who have created these."

B.P. KS3

"Thank you so much. I can't tell you what a help it will be."
A very grateful teacher, Kerryann SA

"...you've certainly got a corner of East Anglia convinced that this is a fantastic way to teach and progress English literature and language!!"
Chris Mehew

"With many thanks again for your excellent resources and upbeat philosophy."

Dr. Marcella McCarthy
Leading Teacher for Gifted and Talented Education,
The Cherwell School, Oxford

"Dear Classical Comics,
Can I just say a quick "thank you" for the excellent teachers' resources that accompanied the *Henry V* Classical Comics. I needed to look no further for ideas to stimulate my class. The children responded with such enthusiasm to the different formats for worksheets, it kept their interest and I was able to find appropriate challenges for all abilities. The book itself was read avidly by even the most reluctant readers. Well done, I'm looking forward to seeing the new titles."

A. Dawes, Tockington Manor School

"I wanted to write to thank you - I had a bottom set Y9 class that would have really struggled with the text if it wasn't for your comics, THANK YOU."

Dan Woodhouse

"As to the resource, I can't wait to start using it! Well done on a fantastic service."
Will

OUR RANGE OF OTHER CLASSICAL COMICS STUDY GUIDES

Henry V	*Macbeth*	*Frankenstein*	*A Christmas Carol*	*Great Expectations*
Published: November 2007	Published: March 2008	Published: October 2008	Published: October 2008	Published: January 2009
Price: £19.99	Price: £19.99	Price: £19.99	Price: £19.99	Price: £19.99
ISBN: 978-1-906332-07-5	ISBN: 978-1-906332-10-5	ISBN: 978-1-906332-37-2	ISBN: 978-1-906332-38-9	ISBN: 978-1-906332-13-6

BRINGING CLASSICS TO COMIC LIFE

Classical Comics has partnered with Comic Life to bring you a unique comic creation experience!

Comic Life is an award-winning software system that is used and loved by millions of children, adults and schools around the world. The software allows you to create astounding comics in a matter of minutes – and it is really easy and fun to use, too!

Through RM Distribution, you can now obtain all of our titles in every text version, electronically for use with any computer or whiteboard system. In addition, you can also obtain our titles as "No Text" versions that feature just the beautiful artwork without any speech bubbles or captions. These files can then be used in Comic Life (or any other

software that can handle jpg files) enabling anyone to create their own version of one of our famous titles.

All of the digital versions of our titles are available from RM on a single user or site-license basis.

For more details, visit www.rm.com and search for Classical Comics, or visit www.classicalcomics.com/education.

**Classical Comics, RM and Comic Life -
Bringing Classics to Comic Life!**

OUR SHAKESPEARE TITLES ARE AVAILABLE IN THREE TEXT FORMATS

Each text version uses the same exquisite full-colour artwork providing a completely flexible reading experience: - you simply choose which version is right for you!

Original Text — THE UNABRIDGED ORIGINAL PLAY BROUGHT TO LIFE IN FULL COLOUR!

Plain Text — THE COMPLETE PLAY TRANSLATED INTO PLAIN ENGLISH!

Quick Text — THE FULL PLAY IN QUICK MODERN ENGLISH FOR A FAST-PACED READ!

Henry V: The Graphic Novel

Published: 5th November 2007 • 144 Pages • £9.99
• Script Adaptation: John McDonald • Pencils: Neill Cameron • Inks: Bambos • Colours: Jason Cardy & Kat Nicholson • Letters: Nigel Dobbyn

Macbeth: The Graphic Novel

Published: 25th February 2008 • 144 Pages • £9.99
• Script Adaptation: John McDonald • Pencils: & Inks: Jon Haward • Inking Assistant: Gary Erskine • Colours & Letters: Nigel Dobbyn

Original Text

ISBN: 978-1-906332-00-6

Original Text

ISBN: 978-1-906332-03-7

Plain Text
ISBN: 978-1-906332-01-3

Plain Text
ISBN: 978-1-906332-04-4

Quick Text

ISBN: 978-1-906332-02-0

Quick Text

ISBN: 978-1-906332-05-1